Finding HOME

Teens Write About Separating from Family and Reconnecting

By Youth Communication

Edited by Laura Longhine

YOUTH
COMMUNICATION
True Stories by Teens

Finding Our Way HOME

EXECUTIVE EDITORS
Keith Hefner and Laura Longhine

CONTRIBUTING EDITORS
Nora McCarthy, Rachel Blustain, Kendra Hurley,
Sasha Chavkin, Sheila Feeney, and Autumn Spanne

LAYOUT & DESIGN
Efrain Reyes, Jr. and Jeff Faerber

COVER ART
YC Art Dept.

For reprint information, please contact Youth Communication.

ISBN 978-1-935552-31-4

Second, Expanded Edition

Printed in the United States of America

Youth Communication ®
New York, New York
www.youthcomm.org

Catalog Item #CW07-1

Table of Contents

Letting the World Back In

> *When the writer returns home after a year in foster*
> *care, she and her mother have become distant, and both*
> *have a hard time trusting people.*

Torn Apart

> *The writer helps his siblings survive on the streets after*
> *being abandoned by their mother. But in foster care, he*
> *is separated from them.*

Loving Letters

> *After years in foster care, Erica and her mother*
> *reestablish a relationship by writing letters.*

Too Far From Mom

> *Chris, who has been placed in a group home, wishes*
> *he lived closer to his mother, even if that means they'd*
> *fight more.*

Going Home Again

> *The writer decides to return home after foster care. But*
> *she finds her dysfunctional family unchanged.*

Contents

Using the Book

Introduction

Separation from biological family is one of the most painful aspects of foster care. Even when parents are neglectful or abusive, being taken from home can be traumatic for children and teens. In this book, young people write about the pain of losing touch with parents and siblings, as well as the complicated emotions of reconnection.

Foster care is meant to be temporary, but it can have a lasting effect on family relationships. In "Paying for the Past," Carmen Caban is happy to welcome her teenage son home, eight years after he went into foster care because of her drug use. But he quickly becomes angry and rebellious, and she doesn't know how to handle it. When families reunite, she writes later, "As parents, we have to deal with our children being angry at us for failing to be someone they could always rely on. Those feelings do not go away easily."

In "Finding Our Way Home" and "It Won't Happen Again," Janelle Allen and her mother Youshell share how family therapy helped them rebuild their relationship, after Janelle and her brother return home from three years in kinship care. As Janelle says:

"Being able to talk out our problems without yelling at one another made a big difference in our lives. We started really listening to each other and I felt that we were gaining back the bond we once had."

And her mother writes:

"As my children saw my persistence in listening to them and in rebuilding our family, it was easier for them to begin to trust me. I felt better, too, as my strength and resolve returned. I told myself, 'I refuse to give up again.'"

Unfortunately, reunification doesn't always end so happily. Angel Fogah writes that she had long felt uncomfortable with her biological mother, and when she is returned home from foster care, things don't improve. "I wanted to be cool with my mom, to hang out and talk, just like she did with my little brother," she writes. "But to me, she always felt like a stranger." Eventually the screaming matches at home get so bad that Angel runs away, and gets placed back in foster care.

Teens who don't officially reunify still have to negotiate a relationship with their biological families. In "Starting Over," Christiaan is thrilled when his mother, with whom he's had only sporadic contact since he entered foster care, texts him and asks to meet for dinner. They have a good time, but a few months later he's still hoping for an apology and an honest discussion about the past before their relationship can really grow.

And in "Going Home Again," Tieysha decides to move back in with her mother and grandmother at age 18, hoping for a new start. But she gradually comes to realize that, even though she's changed, they haven't—and they will probably never be the loving caregivers she's always longed for.

When parents fail, many kids lean harder on their siblings for comfort, love, and caretaking. But all too often, siblings get separated in foster care. And if a sibling gets adopted, those separations can become permanent. In two of the stories in this book, older siblings are devastated to discover that the younger siblings they once cared for have been adopted and cannot be contacted.

Yet sometimes siblings can officially take on a caretaker role. In "A Mother to Me," Roger Griffin and his sister get split up when each is sent to live with a different relative. Although he is placed with an aunt who treats him well, Roger yearns to be with his sister, and keeps running away to be with her. Finally, years later, she is able to officially adopt him. "Living together was so comforting," he writes. "It felt so good to be home."

In the following story, names have been changed: *Going Home Again*.

Skylar Kane Kraemer

Starting Over

By Christiaan Perez

In the four years that I've been in foster care, I have had little to no contact with my mother. I've tried not to show surface signs of the emotions I've been enduring. But I can't recall a time when I went to bed without wondering what my life would be like if I were still living with my mother.

I've asked myself unanswerable questions. "If I stayed home, would my mother keep taking out her anger on me?" "Would I have the same friends?" "Would we get along any better now?"

I thought the daily torment of these questions would never end. I didn't believe I'd ever be able to discuss these feelings with my mother. We'd never held a conversation about our relationship or my feelings. And since four years had passed, and I'm now 18, I wasn't sure I'd ever go home again.

But a few months ago, my mother and I began to communicate. One day soon after I started a summer job, she text-messaged me and asked where I was working. When I told her, she wrote that she worked close by and that she would like to meet me and go out to dinner. I was shocked and thrilled. Once I agreed, I grew anxious. The last time I'd seen her was at a family funeral a year before, and that was for only 10 minutes.

Immediately after work I headed uptown. We'd agreed to meet underneath a big clock facing a small park. On the way over I was thinking to myself, "I hope everything goes well. What are we going to talk about?"

I saw my mom standing under the clock before she saw me. As I approached and she noticed me, she smiled brightly, as did I, and we hugged. All my questions flew out the window. I wasn't worried about anything. I just wanted to enjoy our evening together.

"Are you hungry?" she asked.

"Yeah, I'm ready to eat."

"Good, because I am starving."

We walked up to Times Square, talking about cars, dogs, my job, her job, my sister, how the summer was going for us. It made me very happy to see that she was happy. She was also interested in my job and she asked a lot of questions.

I don't want a polite relationship with my mother. I want her to be my mother and me to be her son.

At the restaurant, we stood on line waiting for a table. I jokingly criticized some of the patrons for being too loud or for not wearing matching clothing, and my mom started laughing, telling me, "Stop," or, "Behave," with a hint of a giggle in her voice.

I'd have bet all of my worldly possessions that when my mother and I finally did meet, there would have been an unbearable awkwardness between us. I expected to be speechless. I was relieved that it felt more like we were old friends, or that she was my older sister, not a mother who had been absent from my life for years.

But later I felt like something was wrong in our conversation. I started to think our discussion could have been between people who were almost strangers. "Am I like that guy from high school that she hasn't seen in years and then runs into on the street? They hold a quick conversation about their lives and then go their separate ways?" I wondered. "Is that who we have become to each other?"

I don't know how parents usually interact with their kids, but I know I don't want a polite relationship with my mother. I want her to be my mother and me to be her son. When I was living at home, my mom and I fought. It was ridiculous. My mother is a professional, accomplished woman, but behind the image she presents to the world, she holds a rage. When I met her anger with my own attitude, we got into shouting matches. Our loudness would rival an arena filled to capacity with excited spectators.

We argued over the smallest things: cleaning my room, walking the dog, and my grades at school. (I was not very fond of school.) There were times when I was a flat-out pain in the ass and deserved what came to me, but mostly it seemed like my mom would just flip unnecessarily. When that happened and I was the target, I barked back.

During these shouting matches, we erupted, slamming doors and throwing random objects. She'd scream hurtful things that I cannot forget: "Why don't you go live with your father?" I fired back primitive commands: "Shut up!" "Leave me alone!"

On too many occasions our shouting turned into physical fights. My mom would go get the belt. Oh, no, I wasn't having that. I wasn't gonna stand still and let anyone hit me. Unwilling to strike back, I did whatever I could to keep myself from being hit. Running, ducking, dodging—not a corner of the house went untouched. This would continue until I locked myself in my room, crippled by a headache or on the verge of losing my voice.

I hated having conflict with my mother. I didn't understand why she had to make it physical, but it seemed unavoidable. She had her mind made up about certain things, and so did I. There was no middle ground. That is a recipe for trouble. But I grew tired of trouble.

Fed up with all the drama, I ran to my grandmother's house when I couldn't take it anymore. Each time, I felt a brief sense of comfort and relaxation. But our confrontations only got worse as our frustration and rage built up. One night my grandmother called ACS, the city's foster care agency, to make a report against my mother. The caseworker decided that I would live with my grandmother until my mother and I worked through our problems.

As much as my mother has hurt me, I admire her, and when we were not speaking I felt sad, lonely, confused, and angry.

At first, the agency mandated that my mother, sister and I go to family therapy once a week. After school my mother would pick us up and take us to the therapist's office. On the way there we usually got along fine, but in the office my mother, my sister, and I would either sit in silence or take turns snapping about what we thought was wrong with each other and why our family had these issues. Coming home we were silent, each of us visibly angry.

Even though the therapist was supposed to help, no good ever came out of those discussions. Disagreeing and yelling at each other only seemed to make things worse. Once the therapy stopped, we mostly stopped talking or seeing each other.

With my mother gone from my life, I felt incomplete. Despite all our conflicts, I admire my mother in many ways, and her values and care have made me who I am today. My mother always held education in high regard. She wanted my sister and me to be intelligent and well-rounded. She made sure we read on a daily basis and practiced our penmanship and mathematics, in and out of school, year round. She made sure we traveled and did activities, like martial arts, to strengthen our minds.

She taught me the value of always looking presentable, and made sure I was well-mannered and capable of holding a conversation with people much older than me. Her insistence led my sister to Exeter, one of the toughest boarding schools in the country, and I also went to boarding school in Pennsylvania last year.

My mother also taught me to assert my authority and never let anyone use me or talk to me like I was inferior. I saw her stand up to whomever raised their voice at her—my father, my grandmother, anyone. Often she took that too far. She was stubborn and refused to lose any arguments. (I did not see it then, but now I see all of these things in myself.)

As much as my mother has hurt me, I admire her, and when we were not speaking I felt sad, lonely, confused, and angry. I felt I'd been left with a gaping hole in the fabric of my life.

I do not blame only my mother for my being in foster care. It takes two people to argue. So I can only hope that we can start over. I'd like us to make up for lost time, if that is possible. I believe my mother has a lot to offer me.

Since that first night when we had dinner, my mom and I have been trying to start a new relationship. We have spoken on the phone, written e-mails back and forth, gone out to dinner, and seen movies.

We have a good time and we enjoy each other's company, but I can't shake the feeling that something is gone between us. Maybe our relationship feels different because I am older and more mature now, or maybe it takes time to make up for so much time apart.

My grandmother has tried to fill a parent's shoes, and now

my mom is trying to be a mother again. But I still feel like I have no parents. My father left long ago, and my mother is not really part of me, either. I think that's because I still don't understand how she feels about everything that went on between us, and she doesn't know how I feel, either.

As long as we are getting along great, I don't want to mess things up by talking about the past. But I hope to someday talk with my mother about what went on between us. I need that to help put our past behind me.

Perhaps one day we will be out to dinner somewhere and one of those "remember the time?" conversations will come up. A conversation that begins with a pleasant, humorous tone will end serious and apologetic, as we pour out everything we have felt.

I'll say, "Remember the time you were in a rush to get to Manhattan and Erika and I were moving really slow? Ha! The train station was right across the street but you were so flustered you walked all the way around the block." We'll laugh, but then the tone will suddenly change as we remember what came next.

My sister and I were standing in front of the house wondering what the hell she was doing walking around the block, and whether she expected us to follow. She arrived back shortly, and shot a glance towards us that said, "Upstairs! Now!"

Once upstairs, she began yelling. "Why are you people holding me up? I have somewhere to be! You think the world revolves around you?" she said.

"You were moving too fast. We weren't ready yet. It's not our fault!" I yelled back.

Our flashback moment will end and, after a few seconds of uncomfortable silence, I'll ask her, "Why would you get so angry at us?"

I can't even imagine what she might say, but I hope that she'll explain her reasons and apologize, and that I'll accept her apology and apologize, too. Over time, with our explanations and apologies we might put the past behind us and enjoy a newfound positive relationship.

Sound like a storybook ending to you? It does to me. But if I could receive an explanation and give one, I think I might be ready to move on. I have been waiting for her explanation for four years, and I have mine prepared.

Christiaan was 19 when he wrote this story.

Sara Goldys

A Mother to Me

By Roger Griffin

For many years my sister was like a mother to me, because our mother was on drugs. Still, we always had food in our stomachs and clothes on our backs. Our mother was the type who made something out of nothing and never complained about life.

So my sister and I didn't worry when our mom was diagnosed with cancer. She seemed healthy and full of life even as she got sicker. When she passed away two years later, my sister and I were hurt beyond belief. We were scared that we had to survive without her.

At the funeral, I felt I had to stay strong and not cry even though everyone around me was crying. I thought of myself as the man of our family, so I held my pain in. But I prayed my mother would wake up and tell me everything was all right.

The first few weeks went by in a daze. My sister and I were

moving like zombies. I was kind of in shock realizing my mother really wasn't coming back.

For the next four months, my sister, her 5-month-old baby and I all stayed in the same apartment we'd lived in with my mother. My sister dropped out of high school to get a job. While she worked our neighbor babysat my niece and me.

My mother always taught us to never let anyone know you're down and out. So we figured we'd survive together with her watching over us. At the time, I didn't understand the danger of living alone in that neighborhood. I didn't really notice that our extended family abandoned us, that we didn't get any visits or phone calls asking if we needed any help. I was too depressed. I couldn't stop thinking about my mother. I shut myself off from the rest of the world, stopped talking to everyone, and wouldn't go outside.

My sister tried to make it seem like everything was normal and fine. It helped that she'd done everything a mother should when we were little, like changing my Pampers and making sure we ate. Every night before I went to sleep, my sister promised me we were going to make it, not only for ourselves but also for our mother.

Being separated from my sister when I had just lost my mother was devastating.

But after four months of living on our own, my sister and I got a visitor we'd never forget— a woman from Child Protective Services. She told us she got an anonymous phone call saying a minor was taking care of two minors in our household.

The woman arranged for my grandmother to move in with my sister and her baby, but since the apartment had only two bedrooms, I was told that I had to move in with my aunt.

Being separated from my sister when I had just lost my mother was devastating. I was homesick at my aunt's. I'd often had fun visiting my aunt, and it was safer for me to be living with an adult, but my sister and I wanted to be together.

21

I got sad and angry, thinking, "I didn't hear from any family members for four months and then, all of a sudden, my grandmother takes my room and I have to move out?" That didn't feel right.

*E*ven though my aunt treated me fairly, I felt that it was her fault that I wasn't at home, and I rebelled against her. Every chance I got I packed a bookbag and ran away to my sister's house. With my sister, I felt safe and comfortable, almost like I still had my mother. But I could never stay. My aunt came and got me every time.

One night after picking me up from my sister's, my aunt was upset. That night she told me what I'd always believed—that she was the one who had called child welfare. I was too young to understand that she did it to protect us, and I never forgave her.

I was hoping that the system would see how much I needed to be with my sister, and would find a way to keep us together.

I told her, "I don't want to talk to you anymore," and I went to my room. After that we never talked.

The last time I ran away, I packed a bag and left at 2 a.m. when everyone was sleeping. A week later the cops came to my sister's house and took me to a holding place for foster youth waiting to be placed in a home. I was hoping that the system would see how much I needed to be with my sister, and would find a way to keep us together. But that day, my aunt went to court and gave up custody of me and I went to a group home in the Bronx.

The first thing staff told me when I got there was, "If you AWOL to your sister's house, we'll have her arrested." I was so afraid that I never even came in after curfew.

Finally, a year later, they moved me to another home that wasn't as strict. I would go to my sister's house and stay two weeks, then stay two days in the group home, then leave again for another two weeks.

When I stayed with my sister we had so much fun. My sister is a big sports fan so we always went to basketball and baseball games. When it snowed, we went outside to play football together. My sister cooked for me, too. One of the things I missed most when we weren't together was the food. There is nothing like a home-cooked meal from my sister.

She was also my role model. She was holding up, taking care of herself and her kids. We always gave each other encouragement when we needed it and made sure we weren't taking ourselves too seriously, either. We made sure we were having fun.

Finally one counselor at my group home noticed how tight my bond with my sister was and decided we belonged together. He suggested that she adopt me. He found an agency and they started the process for us. While we were waiting for it to become official, the group home even allowed me to stay with my sister without getting in trouble.

In 2000, our wish came true and my sister became my guardian. That first night together we played video games all night and reminisced about everything we went through to stay together. We agreed that we were inseparable.

Living together was so comforting. We went to basketball games, and when it snowed we played outside together like old times. It was a relief not having to worry about a group home calling and telling me I couldn't stay with my sister anymore. It felt so good to be home.

Roger wrote this story in a workshop
for Represent *magazine.*

Shamel Allison

Finding Our Way Home

By Janelle Allen

When I was young, life with my mother was good. I loved going to her old job, playing with whatever I could play with and watching her at work. I remember playing hand games with her like "thumb war" and "boom-boom clap-clap." I remember going to day care and not wanting her to leave. I just wanted her to stay with me all day long. No matter how I was feeling, I was always glad to see my mom.

But as I got a little older, it seemed like my mom was always stressed out. My brother was getting into trouble at school and his teachers would call her almost every day. My mother became depressed and tired of having to deal with the same problems all the time.

It wasn't hard to notice because she would complain about whatever made her angry and upset—her job, her kids, or the landlord who wasn't fixing up the apartment. My mother wasn't happy anymore. She always looked sad, like a big cloud was over her shoulder that could rain on her any day.

I didn't understand why she was feeling this way or why she was starting to hate her life so much. All I remember is that things were not good and that I felt like my life would probably never be the same.

I always knew she loved us, but she just had a lot of problems that brought her spirit down. She was having so many problems with my brother's school, and having to go pick him up all the time, that she quit her job. My dad wasn't around, and there is only so much a person can handle. My mother didn't stop doing her duties as a parent, but she basically didn't seem to care anymore about having fun with us and making us laugh.

As the days went on, my mom started getting worse. She'd tell us that she was not doing her best with us and not giving us enough. She thought we needed a better life, and the only person she felt could give that to us was my Aunt Gina, her closest sister.

My mother would call sometimes and ask me if I wanted to come home. I said yes, but I really didn't mean it.

One day a worker from ACS (child welfare) showed up. She had dark skin and hair and she always wore black. My mother didn't like her. Later, I found out that a counselor at my brother's school had called ACS after my mother said she was fed up and couldn't take it anymore.

Even though my mom had been talking about us going to live with Aunt Gina, I wasn't prepared for the social worker to take us away. The day we left, my mother wasn't home, and I had no clue what was going on. I was just scared and wanted the whole thing to be over.

I remember being put in a car that was very uncomfortable. It was a long drive, and I thought that when we got out of the car I would be in front of my aunt's building. That's where I wanted to be. But I was in front of someone else's building.

Luckily, the foster mother was nice, and my brother and I stayed at her home for about a month with no problems. I would get phone calls from my mother from time to time. She'd ask me how I was doing, tell me how much she missed me and how she couldn't wait to see me.

I missed my mom a lot, too. I wondered what she was doing and where she was and what exactly had happened to her that day we were taken away. But I never asked her any of those questions.

After a month, we moved to my aunt's house. Life with my aunt was great. I started going to a new Catholic school and I loved it. My aunt worked there and everyone knew her name.

My mother would call sometimes and ask me if I wanted to see her and come home. Of course I said yes, but I really didn't mean it. I enjoyed being at my aunt's and wanted to stay there forever. I just didn't want to tell my mom that and make her feel bad.

The first time I went to visit my mother I thought I would be happy to see her, but it was kind of weird. I acted like everything was fine, but I didn't feel comfortable talking to my own mother and I wasn't sure why. My mom was so happy to see us and she couldn't stop smiling. We stayed for a little while, then hugged each other and said our good-byes and that was it.

My mother got the chance to visit us on holidays and birthdays, which was great, but I felt more distant towards her, like I didn't want to see her at all. I knew it wasn't right, but that's how I felt at the time. I didn't show it or tell anyone. I just left it alone.

After three years at my aunt's house she told us it was time for us to leave. I couldn't accept the fact that I was going to be going home to my mother and living in the life I'd once left behind. Going back to my past was a slap in the face. I had my life here—my friends, my school, and everything else—and now I had to leave it. That hurt.

It was very hard readjusting to my mother and my new life. My mother seemed so happy to finally have us back. She'd made many changes in her life while my brother and I were gone. I think one of the biggest changes she made was with her anger.

My mother used to get so angry whenever someone would give her attitude. She would yell at the top of her lungs while cussing them out. But since we'd left it seemed like she'd learned how to control that. She seemed calmer, like she was at peace with herself.

Another change was my mom's new boyfriend. When I met him I didn't like him at all. I knew it was wrong to judge a book by its cover, but there was just something about him that convinced me not to trust him.

My mother liked him a lot, though, I could tell, and so did my brother. I felt like an outcast because I was the only one who didn't. My mother noticed and talked to me about it, but I just didn't care. I started not to care about a lot of things that my mother told me to do or not do.

I didn't listen to her or give her any respect. I started talking back and arguing with her all the time. I guess since I'd been gone for a while I thought the only person I should be listening to was my aunt. I knew my mother had the right to give me rules, but I just felt like, "Why should I listen to them?"

My mother didn't know what to do with my brother and me because we were being disrespectful toward her all the time. She said she wasn't going to give up on us again; she was going to find some way to solve this problem. And she did.

She took all of us to family counseling, which I thought was stupid at first. I didn't think it would work.

When we got to our first session I was nervous. I hated being there and I just wanted to leave and go home, but I couldn't. So I sat there and listened to my mother talk to the therapist. Everything she was saying was true. My mom seemed comfortable telling her business, but I wasn't. I didn't know the therapist at all and I didn't feel like telling her anything.

But each time we went I felt more comfortable and open. The therapist was really nice and we each got a chance to say what we were feeling to one another. It took me a while, but once I got to talking I couldn't stop. I told the therapist how I was feeling, the problems I was having with my mom, and everything else about myself. We talked for hours, but I always felt like we didn't have enough time.

As the years went by I started noticing a change in myself as well as my mother. We were getting along much better and talking to each other. And it didn't hurt that she'd gotten rid of that boyfriend.

In therapy, my mother was getting a better understanding of how my brother and I felt and I got a better understanding of how she felt. Being able to talk out our problems without yelling at one another made a big difference in our lives. We started really listening to each other, and I felt that we were gaining back the bond we once had.

Being able to talk out our problems in therapy without yelling at one another made a big difference in our lives.

It's been seven years now since I came home, and my mother and I have a fun relationship. We play around all the time, making jokes and laughing loud and hard at whatever we think is funny. I love my mother a lot and I feel like the older I get the more I appreciate her (even though she doesn't think that).

I love talking to her and I feel she understands me in so many ways, although she still has doubts about me because I don't tell her every little thing. I don't feel comfortable telling her every detail of my social life, but I do feel like I have a better connection with her than I did before.

My mother is a strong woman who has dealt with a lot of challenges in her life and somehow gotten through them. I see her as a person to look up to, even though she doesn't think she is. She tells me all the time that she's made so many mistakes in her life and that I should learn from them.

My mom thinks I don't listen to her when she tells me things, but I am listening in my own little way. I know when I get older I'll look back and know exactly what she meant. Though I don't always show it, I know I'm lucky to have a mother like her.

In the past I felt like I would never be able to forgive my mother for putting me through all this. But now that that I'm older I feel like I can accept the fact that it happened, and move on with my life.

Janelle was 17 when she wrote this story.
Read her mother's story on the next page.

Eric Green

'It Won't Happen Again'

By Youshell Williams

I'd like to share my story. It's not easy for me because I hold my privacy to me like a shield. I fear that I will be judged. But what I'm telling is from my heart. Nine years ago, I lost my two older children to foster care. It took three years for them to come back home. We're still recovering from the pain of that time.

My story begins with my marriage, on July 31, 1989, when I was 19 years old. He was 36 and seemed older and wiser. I wanted someone to love me unconditionally, someone who would appreciate my love. My father was abusive, my mother had died, and I felt lost.

He was my first abuser. I already hated myself, but he made me feel like I was beyond dumb.

God blessed me with a son and a daughter. I did not know a lot about babies, but what I didn't know I lovingly learned. My husband was no help. When he wasn't calling me names, he was out in the streets getting drunk and having affairs.

By 1992 I'd had enough. I let go of my anchor and sent him on his way to give other women hell. After all the chaos and embarrassment my husband had caused me, I didn't miss him.

It wasn't easy taking care of two small children alone, though. Eventually I moved, found childcare, and started looking for a job with the help of a work-readiness program. In 1994 I was hired on a trial basis at a cancer research firm. They liked my hard work and kept me.

Soon I was making good money and had worked my way up to lab technician. I was successful, yet I was not happy. I just did not feel right. I was short-tempered and angry and cried a lot. I didn't know what was wrong with me. I had wonderful support at my job. One nice man suggested that I see a therapist. I didn't listen. I felt I was too strong for that nonsense. Yet I felt myself getting weaker and weaker and crying more and more.

Then things got worse for me at home. The Catholic school my children attended told me my son could not continue on to first grade because he didn't listen and disappeared out of class.

I switched both kids to public school, but their new school was deplorable. The teachers didn't care, and my son was often beaten up by a bully with

My children definitely resented me and the slum they had come home to, and showed it in many ways.

yellow eyes. I rushed to the school from work one day only to be told by the teacher that my son was "around here somewhere." Well, I found him walking down the street, away from the school. At 6 years old! I lost it. I felt my children were being treated like stupid animals, and that reminded me of the way my aunt treated me when I lived with her after my mother died.

That school also had no after-school program, and I worked until 5, so I ended up calling their father and begging for his help. He reluctantly helped out at first, but that didn't last long. He told me, "They're your problem."

Of course, I was soon having lots of problems at work. I was late almost every day; I had to leave early to pick up my children. Finally, I asked my job to lay me off.

Once I stopped working, I became so depressed that some days I wouldn't bother taking my kids to school. I just wanted to keep them home with me where I knew they were safe and taken care of. I was overwhelmed and needed help.

I talked to a social worker at the school and told her, "I can't take it anymore." She didn't ask me what I was talking about, but did take it upon herself to call the abuse hotline and report educational neglect.

An ACS caseworker began coming to my home. She had a very nasty attitude and I refused to bow down to her. Instead I responded in the same nasty way.

A worker from a family support program (called "preventive services" in New York) began visiting, too. She approached me tentatively, in a nice way, but I felt she did not know how to help me. I really did not trust preventive services or know what they were about.

Looking back, I wish I had asked more questions of the preventive worker. I wish I'd asked her to provide me with the services I needed, but I didn't even have a clue what those would be or even how I could help myself.

Eventually, when my son was 6 years old and my daughter was 7, I broke down. One day, after another horrible visit from the demon worker, I called her and asked her to take my children to my sister's house. I thought I was doing the right thing by placing them in foster care.

My son suffered for my mistakes. My daughter suffered for my mistakes. And I suffered, too. I feel I will never forgive myself for giving up.

After my kids went into care, I just barely kept living. The first month was terrible, because the worker put them with a stranger instead of with my sister, until a judge ordered them moved. I was so scared and angry when I didn't know where my children were.

For a short time, I was hospitalized to deal with my depression. Then I went to support programs and worked so I'd have money to give my sister for my kids. I only had two good reasons—my kids—to keep trying.

My children were with my sister for three years. My sister was wonderful. She did above and beyond what a sister or aunt should do. She loved my children. She had her own son, and she treated all three like they were one big happy family.

When I visited my sister's house, I was able to witness the attention she lavished on them. Her caring for my children and me was amazing. I am truly lucky and blessed.

But the separation took its toll. As time passed I became afraid to get my children back, afraid to fail again. Seeing what my sister could provide made me fear that I would mess up my children's lives if I took them back. I lived in a dump. The apartment was nasty, the landlord was a slumlord.

My sister and her husband did not live in the ghetto. They lived in a nice neighborhood with better stores nearby, better schools, better everything. I had high hopes for my children, and still do. I wanted my children to experience the good side of life. I did not want them to become totally ghettofied.

I realized that we may not be able to get those three years back, but we can move forward and make new memories.

I knew my children needed my love and my parenting, and I knew they had more in my house than I ever had growing up. But I believed my children were happy and might think, "Then Mommy came and messed everything up once again." Life felt like one big messy hell for me. It was easier, and somehow felt right, to give up and let someone else do the work of raising them. But my heart sure felt empty.

My sister woke me up. One day she said to me, "It doesn't seem like you want them back." My new worker helped, too. She explained what steps to take to get my children home. Without her, I believe my case could've dragged on forever.

Soon I went to court and I filed a document asking the system to release my children to me. Soon enough, my children came home.

After such a long absence, though, it took a long time for my children and me to get back in the groove. There was tension in our house. My kids acted like I was no longer the parent, Aunt Gina was. (I felt like they were thinking, 'Mommy showed how weak she could be.' Now the respect was gone.)

My son was especially angry, and it was hard for me to help him. His attitude was "life sucks," and I totally agreed with him. Above all, he did not want to face the new man in my life, my future tormenter and second hell, and the new reason for ACS to return to my life years later...but that's another story.

My children definitely resented me and the slum they had come home to, and showed it in many ways: lots of arguments, disrespect and shouting that "You should have left us at Aunt Gina's!" Plus a whole lot of pretending that they did not hear me or my rules.

Thank God, about a year later we moved into a much nicer apartment where my children each got their own rooms. The move eased the tension some, but Mommy still didn't get respect from her children. And when my son and daughter visited Aunt Gina on the weekends, forget about it. When they came home on Sunday nights, the anger on their faces was chilling. I'd get angry, too, and just say, "Yeah, y'all home now, so go unpack and get ready for school tomorrow."

"Yeah, whatever!" they'd say, slamming their doors. Sometimes I would hear one or the other muttering to themselves, "I wish I could have stayed at Aunt Gina's!"

Luckily, I was required to go to a preventive agency when my kids returned home, and the agency we were sent to was very good. My worker was nice and understanding. She helped me with my son by joking with him and trying to draw him out of his shell, and by going out to his school to talk with his teachers, because he was always having difficulties.

She was great, and when she left after two years, I found another agency. I loved my second worker. She started us on family therapy and I was hooked. Every week we went to her office to talk with her as a family. My favorite part was a game where we all had to say words that expressed how we were feeling at that moment, and how we felt about each other.

I found out a lot. My children were fearful and disappointed in me. I had seemed so strong to them that it had been shocking to them to watch me fall so hard. They were bitter and scared that I might fall once again. They wanted to stay with Aunt Gina because she showed strength consistently and they could trust her.

How my children felt was very important to me, but at home all I heard was their anger. When we played the

For a long time, I didn't think that I deserved my children, but now I know that no one else can be a better mother to them.

games, I was able to hear them express their fears and frustration, and what they wanted from me. I realized that my children had cause for concern, and their fear wasn't just that I would fail in the future, but that our family would not recover from the past. They were asking, "Where do we go from here?"

I was determined to put their fears to rest by telling them and showing them that Mommy would never give up on herself again. I also realized that we may not be able to get those three years back but we can move forward and make new memories, happier memories.

Family therapy has helped. Our worker encouraged us to keep building our trust in each other. She'd say, "Change can be a good thing. It helps you grow as a family."

As my children saw my persistence in listening to them and in rebuilding our family, it was easier for them to begin to trust me. I felt better, too, as my strength and resolve returned. I told myself, "I refuse to give up again."

I don't know how completely my children trust me now, but we are more comfortable with each other and we have come a long way. Despite the obstacles that still insist on blocking our paths, we are struggling through together, as a family.

It would have been easy, in the face of their hostility, to just quit, throw my hands up, and say, "Y'all don't need me." But that wasn't true. They needed me to be their advocate, to talk to them, and most of all, to be their caring mother. For a long time, I didn't think that I deserved my children, but now I know that no one else can be a better mother to them.

Now, when my children return from visiting Aunt Gina, they come home saying, "Hi, Mom." I say, "Hello" with a smile. They're not angry and I'm not angry. I'm happy to see them, and I see in their faces now that they are happy to be back. These days, when they go to their rooms, they no longer slam the doors.

Youshell wrote this story for Rise, *a magazine by and for parents involved in the child welfare system. Reprinted with permission. www.risemagazine.org*

Gabriel Mateo

Family Therapy:
A Safe Place to Connect

Adrienne Williams-Myers, program director of Project Safe at the Northside Center for Child Development in New York City, explains how therapy can support reunifying families.

Q: How can therapy help families reconnect?

A: When parents and kids are involved in the system, their world has been full of other people telling them what to do. Therapy is a time for them to focus on themselves and their goals. I help families identify their strengths, resilience, and love for each other, and to really work on enhancing those strengths so they can stay together.

By learning how they overcame the troubles that led to their separation, families can use their strengths to get through the confusing emotions and tensions that come with reunification.

Q: What do parents and kids often feel when they've been separated?

A: The parent usually comes in feeling a tremendous amount of guilt because she didn't do what she needed to do to prevent children from being removed. Mothers may also blame the system or the school system for making the call, or blame the other parent or relatives that didn't support her.

Sometimes mothers still feel angry that the way they punished their children was considered abuse. Many times they will tell us, "My mom hit me, my teachers hit me. What's the problem? I'm fine."

For the children, there's a lot of anger and anxiety about ending up back in care again. The little ones, especially, feel a lot of separation anxiety. They're anxious and fearful that the system will take them away again, and they've lost trust in their parents' ability to protect them.

> *For children, there's a lot of anger and anxiety about ending up back in care again.*

Older children tend to be angry and to blame the parent. They need a period of time to get to know the parent again and to feel comfortable trusting the parent. If substance abuse issues led to the child going into foster care, they need to be sure that mom is not picking up again.

Q: What are some techniques that help parents and kids get to know each other?

A: In family therapy, I help them get to know and trust each other, mostly by allowing them simply to talk and hear each other. Sometimes I ask them to write feelings or experiences down in journals, or to talk into a tape recorder and then listen to themselves. I ask them to watch each other communicate, including all forms of communication: words, body language, hugging, and kissing.

I'll ask them things like, "How do you see yourself positively? How do you think mom or teacher sees you positively? Or how do you think your child sees you positively? Tell me six great things about yourself." I'll ask them to write it down and share it with each other. Sometimes they're kind of shocked to find out that mom sees them in a positive light, or that the other people in their family notice the same positive things.

At some point, I'll also ask the kids to say what they went through in foster care to help their parents understand that painful time. If it's too upsetting, they can write it down and hold it for a while before sharing it, or even mail it.

> *Therapy can help make a safe place for everyone in the family to express themselves, especially to express the anger in a healthy way.*

Therapy can help make a safe place for everyone in the family to express themselves, especially to express the anger in a healthy way. It's better if children and parents don't hold that anger inside or express it in blowups.

Therapy can also help moms work on the behaviors that will help their children trust them again. A parent who was using drugs or drinking usually was in the habit of making false promises and not following through. Moms can learn how to be there for their kids by making only the promises they can follow through on. Becoming a trusting family again really happens one day at a time.

Shamel Allison

Letting the World Back In

By Anonymous

When my brother and I first came home, everything had changed: the furniture, the TV, the bed in my room, even the kitchen floor was different. But it didn't really matter, because we were home.

My brother and I had just come back from a year in foster care, where we had lived in five or six different places. The day we finally came home, I don't think I knew what to feel. But my mom was happy.

Soon after we got home, my mom had a talk with my brother and me. She explained why they took us, and how she fought to get us back. My mother told us that after we'd been taken away she couldn't stand to be in the house without us, so she took a vacation and when she came back she redecorated the whole house. She also explained that when the agency had said she didn't want to see us anymore, it was a lie.

She said she was sorry for missing my birthday but since my next birthday was only a couple of weeks away she was going to throw me a party. That kinda made me feel home again, because she'd always thrown me a party since I was one year old.

But being back at home did feel a little strange. It was hard to feel comfortable again, and not misplaced. I had been taken away from everything that made me feel safe and relaxed, and then a year later put back where I started. But in the meantime, I had changed.

I'd learned to be more aware of things around me, when people think I'm not paying attention. I realized the world changes every day, and there are some people you can trust and some you can't, and you can't always tell the difference. I guess that was the start of me keeping to myself and worrying about every little thing.

Even now, six years after we came home, I still don't trust people as much as I would like to. I don't think I'm ready to let someone back in after all that pain—not even my mother.

I guess you could say my mom and I became distant because of what happened. We did talk about my experiences in foster care, but it was very uncomfortable for me because I went through it and I wanted to forget it all and never talk about it again.

I wanted to forget being in care and never talk about it again.

Our year in foster care had changed my mom, too. She was always worried that ACS (child welfare) would be knocking at the door again. We couldn't do things the way we used to, like rough-housing around the house.

From that day on she became more and more protective of us. She didn't trust the world. Everywhere she went we had to be right by her side or she would flip, and that's continued to this day.

Like when we go shopping for clothes she has to come, even

though the mall isn't that far from our house. Everywhere she goes, we go, every street, every turn, there we are. I feel like a puppy walking in step with its master.

Now that I'm a teenager, it's getting on my nerves. I want to be able to be by myself without having to know she's right there. It's frustrating because I feel like she doesn't understand certain things about me, like that I have to be my own person in this world and she can't smother that growth.

But we don't see eye to eye, so we can't really talk it out. When I tell her I'm not a baby she starts saying she knows that, and then goes on about how the world is dangerous.

I think she's still affected by my brother and me having been put in care, and the fact that we are getting older probably means for her that she can't protect us as much as she wants to. She's trying to keep me closed from what's really out there. But I feel like I am willing to take the risk now to be in a world that is dangerous. I can't hide from it.

And I hope when she sees that I can do things on my own, without having to look over my shoulder and worry, she will take that deep breath and let go.

The author was 16 when she wrote this story.

Walter Moore

Torn Apart

By Anonymous

Carried nine months by a drug-addicted mother, I was born into a house where I was only as good as her next fix. I don't know what neighborhood we lived in. I only remember the reeking smell of piss in the hallway of our project, leaks in the ceiling, cracks in the wall, no heat in the winter and no AC in the summer. My little brother and sister and I slept on the floor because we had no bed to call our own. Our fridge was as empty as a poor man's pocket. Our mother never cooked for us; we survived on the scraps of food that she left.

Stepping on needles and glass in my mom's old apartment, the cuts on my feet bled like the scars from my heart. I wanted my mother to love me, but her addiction consumed her. It was more powerful than her love for her own kids.

As a young child I wasn't aware that my surroundings were

unusual. People were getting mugged and beaten in the stairwell, so the cops stayed in our building like it was a police station. And in our home, drugs were an everyday object. There was nothing shocking about it, and when I think back on the other kids in our building, I realize that we weren't the only ones suffering with a parent's addiction. But at the time I was unafraid, because this life was all I knew.

As I got older, the greed of my mother's addiction grew. When she could not get her fix, or when she was forced to go sober from the lack of cash, she would hit us with a broomstick, extension cord, or anything else that she could get her hands on. She was desperate to find some way to forget about her own problems, something that would give her a rush.

My brother and sister and I became closer than the average siblings because we had to look out for each other in order to survive. In the beginning there wasn't much I could do to protect them from my mom's abuse. I couldn't even protect myself. But we would do little things to try to comfort

My brother and sister gave me something to believe in when I didn't think we'd make it.

each other. Like if my sister was beaten, I would take the leftover food and give it all to her.

Then, when I was 7, my mother's addiction got so bad that she could not support her habit and maintain an apartment. She got evicted, and we followed her to a shelter in Brooklyn. The shelter was scary. I remember people stealing from each other.

I don't know how much time passed, maybe a few weeks. But one warm day, we went out with our mother and she just walked away from us. We didn't follow her, because we thought that she would be coming back. But she never did. After a while, we started getting hungry. We didn't know what to do. We didn't know how to get back to the shelter. That's when survival mode kicked in.

I'd never been able to depend on my mother, so I didn't really miss her when she disappeared. My main concern was getting us something to eat. When it got dark, we started walking. When we saw the projects, I thought we were home, but they weren't the same ones we'd lived in with our mom. We didn't know were else to go, so we followed someone into the building, cuddled up together on the floor and went to sleep.

From that day on, we were on our own on the streets. Like animals in the wild, we had to adapt to our environment. There were many nights we went hungry so we stole food, slept on the sidewalk and begged for money. But when people would just pass by, it made me cold-hearted. I felt no love, no joy, no happiness toward or from those who walked by.

I started to feel helpless, but besides that, my feelings were very limited. Except toward my brother and sister. They were a warm part of my heart, just a different part of me. Only they held the keys to my emotions.

We lived in filth, totally alone on the street. We had nothing but the clothes on our backs, which also served as blankets as it got colder. We would wash ourselves in the McDonald's bathroom sink. Sometimes we'd even sleep in restrooms at McDonald's, Burger King or other fast food restaurants. Sometimes customers would kick us—literally kick us—to get us out of the restroom. As far as I know, no one ever checked to see if we had an adult looking out for us. Sometimes we'd lock ourselves in the restroom to sleep for a while, and the employees would unlock the door with their keys. Again, no one asked if we had a parent. They just told us to leave and sent us back out into the street.

Other times we'd take shelter inside the projects. We'd wait in the shadows and after a person entered the building, one of us would quietly come forward and hold the door. The other two of us would run in and we'd spend the night on the stairs or in the hallway. It really wasn't any better than sleeping in the restroom at McDonald's, because the stairs were full of places where people had pissed. We'd have to find a place to lie down where there was no piss, but the smell still invaded our air and made it difficult to sleep. And when winter came, it was cold sleeping on the floor.

We went to different stores each night to steal food, moving carefully so we wouldn't be noticed. We'd put the food items in our pants and shirts, and while the cashier was dealing with a customer, we'd walk out.

We couldn't steal from McDonald's and KFC, so we'd wait till the end of a shift when they dumped food out and we ate out of the garbage. This was very dangerous, because we were competing with other homeless people, mainly adults, who hadn't eaten in days.

At first, it was hard to let go of the past. As rough as our lives had been before, I still had hope of finding our mom. But after a while I had to give up the past. If you don't stay focused on the present in circumstances like that, you're setting yourself up for failure, because you're distracted from what needs to happen right now in order to survive. Getting caught wasn't an option.

I didn't realize that the only thing that kept me strong, my siblings, would be taken away from me.

I never saw caring for my siblings as a short-term responsibility. I took it as a permanent responsibility, in place of a mother and father. I was the authority, but we needed each other to survive. They depended on me to make strategies and come up with plans for how we were going to eat and where we were going to sleep, to find something to wear and to protect them. I depended on them for motivation, which helped me protect not only them but myself.

My brother and sister gave me a strong will and something to believe in when I didn't think we'd make it. They helped me find courage; I had to be strong for them. When I had a cold heart, they kept me warm inside. For their sake, I learned to numb my feelings when I was hurting. This was important, because if I had spent time getting attached to other people, or feeling hurt when other people mistreated us, I wouldn't have had the energy to keep going. Instead, I just focused on my brother and sister, and did everything for them. That was how I survived.

For months we lived this way, until my brother got caught stealing one summer day. His ribs were sticking out, dried spit crusted on his mouth from dehydration, wearing two different shoes on his feet and no shirt. The sun's heat blazed on his skin as he ran out of a nearby corner store with stolen goods.

The patrolman spotted him running down the street with one kids' size 11 boot and another size 6 toward the building where my sister and I were waiting. The door was cracked, and when my brother went to open the door he got caught. That's when the patrolman discovered the rest of us and we got pulled into the system.

When they explained what would happen to us next, I was relieved. We were going to have clean clothes, food and a roof over our heads. I felt like I was in heaven, but little did I know that the physical and mental abuse would regenerate itself.

We lived in a group home for children for a while and were then placed in foster home after foster home, about 12 altogether. A lot of these homes were physically abusive. I remember that they'd treat their own kids good while they'd smack and hit us—sometimes with belt buckles—and tell us we weren't worth nothing.

Finally, when I was about 13, we found a good foster home. Our foster mother showed us love and compassion. She never called us nasty names or beat on us.

I wasn't used to kindness from an adult, because I'd been abused all my life. I couldn't let her love me. Her love felt different, it felt like something was missing. In fact, something was being gained, but I couldn't see it at the time. I'd never known an adult to give me love.

My foster mother finally had to let me go because I kept pulling away and her love couldn't hold me. Abuse had broken my heart into a million pieces and she tried to pull it together, like a puzzle. But my hatred for my past foster families who abused me and used me for the money made me sink like an anchor and I drowned in sorrow.

She couldn't handle me, so I was moved to another foster home. It was a good home, but I tried to sabotage it because I just wanted to be back with my siblings. I'd start fires, or drink too much alcohol so that the ambulance would have to come and take me to the hospital.

My law guardian explained that my siblings had been adopted by my former foster mother, so their file was confidential.

My behavior finally caused me to be placed in a residential treatment center. I didn't realize that the only thing that kept me strong, my siblings, would be taken away from me. If I'd known, I would have done anything in my power to keep them in my life.

At first I kept in touch with my brother and sister. But one day, about six months after I moved to the RTC, I called our old foster mother, who they still lived with, and no one called me back. I called again and the answering machine said they no longer lived there. I was so shocked and disturbed. Why would someone want to keep me away from my brother and sister?

As I got older, I tried to find a way to contact them, but I got nowhere. My law guardian explained that they'd been adopted by my former foster mother, so their file was confidential. They weren't allowed to give me any information about my brother and sister. I was hurt. I continued trying to find them by looking up their names and the foster mother's name on the computer, but I had no luck.

In the process of writing this story, I suddenly realized that my brother and sister are now teenagers. It was the first time I'd thought of them that way; in my mind, they were still children.

When I realized they were teenagers, my first thought was, "That's crazy." I started thinking about my sister with a boyfriend and how I would act. How would I explain to my little brother about protecting himself and practicing safe sex? How would they manage without me there as a positive authority figure? Who did they call on when they needed help?

I also wonder if they think about me. I want to know if they miss me, if they feel the same way about me as I feel about them. Knowing that they're alive gives me hope, but not knowing what's going to happen to them worries me very much. If they died, I wouldn't even know. If I found out years later, me not being there would hurt me even more.

My childhood was nonexistent, and I can never get it back. Too young, I had to face the cold reality of the streets. Even though I'm 19 now, I can't help but let out the inner child sometimes. I try to be serious, but my vibe and my energy change the mood with people around my age. Some people think there's something wrong with me, but I'm just trying to get back something that was taken.

The picture in my mind is still of my brother and sister with me, frozen in our childhood years. I haven't been able to put an updated picture in the frame. I dwell on my childhood, always wondering about what I was like as a kid. The only two people who shared those times were my brother and sister. Without them, I'll never have a complete picture of who I was then.

The author was 19 when he wrote this story.

Gabriel Mateo

Loving Letters

By Erica H.

I didn't have much family growing up, but once I hit my teenage years my mother and father were just a letter away. They kept a place in my heart by sending me their love in writing. Do I feel grateful that I have both of my parents sending me their love each week? You bet I do. When I get their letters I find hope.

My father's letters remind me that he has always been in my life. Even though he did not have custody, he sent money and stayed in touch, even if it was just a phone call, a letter, or a visit here and there.

My dad sends encouraging notes like this one:

>I will just be glad when the three of us can get together again. I am working on that. Please hang in there and don't lose faith in me.

My mother and I use letters to catch up on lost time and heal from our painful pasts together. For years my mother and I had lost contact completely. I was taken from her as a young child, and then again when I was 12. (My dad split from the family when I was little.) I've been in foster care since then, and during that time she lost her rights in court.

But last year I wrote a story for Youth Communication and sent it to her in the mail. My story described the two years I spent in a mental hospital as a child, and my struggles to deal with the effects of my mother's explosive temper and drug abuse. I also wrote about nights I spent sleeping in the hallway of our building, which led to me getting sexually assaulted.

Even though the story described the pain I went through, I sent it to my mother so she could see how well I was

I still wanted my mother to be a part of my life, despite the mistakes she made raising me.

doing, and to show her how proud I was of my writing. I wanted to let her know that I still wanted her to be a part of my life despite the mistakes she made raising me.

I was unsure if it was a good idea to be in touch. The court demanded that my mother stay away from me, and I feared that if the judge found out that my mother was back in my life, I'd be in trouble.

But taking the risk was worth it. When my mother wrote back, I felt like a piece of my broken heart was repaired and a part of my pain was wiped away.

In my letters since then, I've let my mother know that I am not angry at her for what I went through in foster care, but I am angry at her for not taking care of her responsibilities. It was hard for her to support two kids, but everybody struggles and that isn't a reason to skip out on your kids. I also let her know that I appreciate that she is now trying to make up for the bad things she did.

From my mom's letters, I've found out that she went through similar experiences to mine. She wrote:

I am very proud of you. I can't believe I lived to see our daughter in the youth magazine telling true stories. I'm sorry I had to hear about our young lady being abused and raped as a child. All my life I was being abused and raped also. PS—Keep up the good work writing stories and letters.

Another time she wrote:

You are a good writer. I hope you're in the next issue. I understand that it hurts to talk about the past, because it hurts to remember the pain. The courts have demanded that I face my fear. I've been sent to support groups for sexual abuse, and for handling rejection and abandonment. All of us hate to talk about these painful problems.

Reading her letters, I was glad that my mother could understand my pain growing up. I felt less alone knowing we'd been through similar things.

Writing to my mother also has given me a better insight into why she used to drink and become angry and violent when I was younger. She had her own problems to deal with on top of mine. Knowing her struggles, I felt I could forgive my mother and feel less hurt and anger, and that we could build a better bond together.

Soon my mother sent another letter, this time about anger. Like my mom, I struggle with blowups:

…Don't let nobody or no one push your buttons. Your mom and dad, we both have hot tempers, short fuses. If you find yourself getting anger problems—count to 10, think first. Use writing to get inside your heart and soul. Every day write a line saying something good about yourself.

My mother's tips actually work! I've been trying to follow those tips rather than react in a violent manner when someone ticks me off. I was proud to see that my mom is working on her anger, too.

My mother seems to feel sad about the way she parented me when I was a kid. She wrote:

> Dear Erica, I hope you're doing fine. I miss you...I tried to be a good mother....I love you for being a nice daughter.
> I'm happy for your new life. When you grow up to be a mother one day try to be better than me. Remember to set rules for your children. Hugs and kisses, Your mother.

She told me to set rules for children (when I have them) because she didn't do that with my sister and me. We had no curfew, chores, or discipline. That caused me to become out of control. She set no rules partly because she was checked out, but my mother also wanted us to have the freedom she didn't

Knowing her struggles, I felt I could forgive my mother and feel less hurt and anger, and that we could build a better bond together.

have growing up. I get the impression that my grandmother didn't play no games.

Despite enduring a lot of violent behavior when I was living with my mom, I also experienced painful things living in foster care. Sometimes I feel I would have been better off with my mother. At least my mother has always loved me. She expresses that a lot in her letters.

She wrote:

> Hello, Erica, Just a few words to say I love you, I'm doing fine...

And:

> I love you and Nicole [my sister] with all my heart and soul. The real world is different than

living in the Bronx. Please remember to write
back...

I loved how she told me, "The real world is different than living in the Bronx." She meant that when we lived there, everywhere you turned there was trouble. It was like a trap that led to failure.

Now my mother has reunited with my father in New Jersey and she's sober and taking care of herself. My father has changed, too, and he saves my mother from failing. She needs my father to look after her and make sure she doesn't slip.

I am proud of my mother! She has grown a lot. She's laying low in the home, writing me letters and being the mother that I always wanted: loving, giving and helpful, just like me.

I have grown a lot as well. My lifestyle was once about being with different boys and running the streets. Now I am stable, living on my own with my boyfriend. I found the courage to change.

I did go through a lot in the past with my mother, but I'm hopeful now that we're both growing together, getting to know one another and dealing with our problems head on.

Erica was 20 when she wrote this story.
She later married and had two children.

Too Far From Mom

By Chris Brooks

Because my mother and I used to fight so much, she put me in a group home in San Fransisco. But even after I moved, we continued to fight, so they moved me to a group home farther away from her, and then they moved me again, even farther away than that. Even though we fought so much, I miss her now, and I wish that I lived closer to her.

My mom first called the cops on me on December 13th, my brother's birthday, an unlucky day. That was a day I went kind of crazy on my mother.

That morning, I started to argue with my mom and my mom said she was going to whip me. I got mad. She started to yell at me and I started to yell back and I began to cry. I thought about all the times she'd hit me. She'd hit me with extension cords. She'd hit me with metal hangers. She'd pull my hair. She'd hit me with her knuckles on my head. I used to say, "When I get older, she won't do that to me anymore." But now she was threatening to do it again.

I remembered all that and I balled up my fists and put them up in a threatening manner. I don't remember much right after that because then I blacked out. I couldn't see anything but I knew I was moving. I didn't feel anything but that I was moving and going crazy. It's like I went into another world. When I came back into focus, my mom was on top of me holding my arms down on the couch. I was trying to get her off me but she was too strong for me to budge.

I miss the times when my mom and I got along and didn't fight.

She called to my brother and said, "Call the cops," and my brother ran into the other room and called while my mom was still on top of me. When the cops came, a female cop took me into my room.

The cop told me, "Stop acting up or you'll get yourself in juvenile hall."

She also said something that stuck with me. The cop said my mom was intimidated by me. I was kind of happy when I heard that. I was happy because my mom just always hit me and finally I had stood up for myself.

After that, we continued having problems. My mom kept yelling at me so I yelled at her back and then I'd run away. I'd spend the night at my friend's house. My mom would call the cops on me and I would have to go home to her house. After that, my mom would not talk to me for several days, but soon we'd start fighting again. Finally my mom couldn't take me anymore and she put me in a group home.

I was only in that home for a little while and my mom came to visit me two times. I was getting physically abused in the group home so I told my mom about it and she took me back home. At first I was very happy, but after a little while I felt more pissed at my mom than before and I acted up more. I was out of control. I was running away, fighting with my brother, fussing with my mom, banging on the walls when I was mad. I threatened my brother several times and punched him and threw things at him, too. After that, my older brother did not like me for a good while. He's a mama's boy and he was scared of me. I didn't want my brother to be afraid of me, but when I got angry I didn't think about what I was doing.

Within three months I was back in a group home. My mom would come and visit once every two weeks. Sometimes we would fight during the visits. We'd fuss about my behavior and about when I could come home again. I would get extremely mad and start yelling at my mom and she would start yelling at me, too.

Eventually they moved me farther away from my mom because we were fighting so much, and then they moved me again. Right now I live in San Fransisco, about a three-hour drive from her.

I don't miss our fights. But I do miss some of the things she used to do to show me she loved me during the times when we were getting along.

When I was little, I remember how she used to pick me up and hold me when I got hurt. Sometimes she would baby me and tickle me. She'd read us stories and bake us chocolate cake and chocolate chip cookies. When she baked, I used to try to eat all the cookies. (Sometimes she would whip me for that.) Once my mom took my brother and me to Sea World with my aunt to see all the whales. That's a nice memory.

I miss the times when my mom and I got along and didn't fight. Not having my mother around or having any kind of mother in my life today makes me feel sad and lonely, like there's no one who cares for me. Being so far from my family sometimes makes me feel like even my mother and brother don't care.

It's also hard because when I'm having trouble with staff or other people in the system, I can only call my mom, but I can't go see her and she can't come see me and stick up for me in person. I know that if she was closer, she would do that for me.

Now I see my mom and my brother just on the holidays, and sometimes when we go stay with my aunt. When I go to my aunt's, I have lots of fun with my cousins. We crack jokes and make each other laugh. I feel happier then than almost any other time.

Before, when I was hanging with my cousins, I used to talk all the time about how fat my brother was to make my cousins laugh. But one time last year I took the time to talk to my brother and say I'm sorry for talking about him all these years and for the times I beat him up, too.

When I said that, he said, "That's OK," and then he kind of smiled. I felt a little better after that. We haven't fought since then. I feel like if I had a chance to see my brother and talk to him more about my feelings, then our relationship would improve even more.

If my mom apologized, it would seem like she wanted to change, and that would make me want to change.

I haven't apologized to my mother. I don't feel like apologizing to her until she apologizes to me for whupping me so much when I was younger. She did me wrong, too, and I'm still angry. If my mom apologized, it would seem like she wanted to change, and that would make me want to change. I wish we could work things out because I don't want to fight anymore. It doesn't get me anywhere but trouble and I know I need to change my behavior.

If we lived closer, maybe we'd just fight more. I fight with her now whenever I ask her to take me home and she says no. But if I lived closer to her, maybe we would have more of a chance to talk. I could ask my mom more about how she feels about me and I could tell her how I feel about her. Then we might be able to work something out. Since I'm older, I would try to talk to her with a level tone and hold my tongue when I wanted to say something smart.

I do think things might get worse because we argue loud and hard, but I'd rather be screaming and yelling at her than being so far away. Right now I don't feel like I have anyone who can relate to me, who knows what I like, who I can bond with. Right now there's no one here who gives me a mother's love. My mom and my brother are my family. Being so far away makes me feel all alone.

Chris was 19 when he wrote this story.

Karolina Zaniesienko

Going Home Again

By Tieysha

I was 20 when I left care. I was in a residential treatment center and was having lots of difficulties with the rules. I left placement one night. When I returned, the director of my facility said, "Maybe you shouldn't come back." She said I had always isolated myself from the other residents. I had, because I didn't want to get involved with things some of the other residents were doing, like drugs, drinking, fighting, breaking house rules, and not going to school. I wanted to be successful in life.

My house director said, "I can place you in another group home for the last few months that you're here." I thought, "Why start over?" So I returned home. Even though I had gone to all of my independent living workshops, was working and in college, going home was still what I always had in the back of my mind.

The problem was that I returned to a home environment

that had never really changed. It was one of those choices that I shouldn't have made. It's damaged me in a lot of ways. Most of the setbacks I've had since I left care were really due to my family. Being home again made it hard for me to have my mind clear to make positive choices.

When I was young, I didn't have a good relationship with my family, but they always taught me that I should never go against family. I was brainwashed into believing that my family was always going to protect me, and I thought it was my job to protect them.

That's why, when I came into care, I did not talk about anything that was going on with my family. I have a cousin who's 7 years older than me. When I was a kid, he was put in charge of me. Sometimes he would hit me. He shouldn't have been allowed to. But if I complained to my mother, she'd say, "So what if he hit you? He's family."

There was sexual abuse that was overlooked, too. The sexual abuse started when I was 4 and continued until I was 12. A cousin knew and didn't say anything. My mother found out when I was 12 and I wrote a story about it, but she just kind of blanked it out.

My mother and grandmother are both functional alcoholics, but I never talked about the alcoholism or its affect on me, either.

I didn't like being in care, but being away from my family helped me focus on my own needs.

I had a drinking problem myself when I was in high school. My mother would tell me, "I don't ever want to see you out drinking on the street. If you drink, I want you to do it at home." So I'd say, "I want a 40 ounce," and my mother would go buy it for me. (I don't blame her for that. We both were weak with troubles.)

For a long time, I didn't talk about any of these things because my first loyalty was to my family. Eventually, though, I did begin to open up. Three and a half years after I came into care, I told a teacher, and then a social worker, about the alcoholism in my family. I began to talk about some of the other problems, too.

I didn't like being in care, but being away from my family helped me focus on my own life and figure out my own needs. I was eventually enrolled in Alateen, which is a program for teens who have alcoholic relatives. There they helped me to stop drinking and find better ways to cope with my emotions.

Being away from my family also helped me in practical ways. I went into care because the problems at home led me to run away and cut school. But by the time I left the system, I was in college and working as a clerical worker and a nurse's assistant at Harlem Hospital. I also volunteered with the homeless and with battered women, and was involved in a number of church groups. All these things made me feel good about myself.

The problem was that while I had begun to change, my family wasn't changing. At the time, that was too hard for me to realize. When I finally left care, I thought that since I'd gotten my life more together, I could go home and make everything OK with my family, too.

When I returned home, I really wanted it to work. I moved in with my mother, who lives upstairs in a private house, while my grandmother lives below. For a short while, we had a honeymoon period. But soon, my mother and I began fighting again.

Our fights upset me so much that they affected my life outside the home. If I'd had a bad argument with my mother, I'd still get up and go to college the next day, but my mind was so stressed that I wouldn't be able to focus. I had to take a semester off because my grades were so badly affected. I also didn't make as many career advances as I would have liked. Instead, I got lost in my family. I forgot who Tieysha was and what Tieysha needed to be doing.

One year after I left care, my mother kicked me out of the house because of the same old problems. I went to live with my aunt for two or three months, but then the same cousin who'd been in charge of me when I was younger threw me out of my aunt's house. That night I moved back into my mother's house, this time into the basement apartment.

When I moved back in with my mother, I felt so low. I wanted to be a part of my family, but they kept letting me down—first my mother kicking me out and then my cousin. I didn't feel like it was ever, ever going to get better.

That day I called a good friend in Seattle, Dennis, and told him that I felt burnt out and hopeless. He said, "Don't feel that way. If you want, you

I thought that since I'd gotten my life more together, I could go home and make everything OK with my family, too.

can come to Seattle and live with me. You can do nothing or you can do everything. It's up to you."

But when you're as connected to your family as I was, it's very hard to make that break. Even when you can see how badly the relationships are affecting your life, it's hard to turn your back on them when they're the only family you've ever known.

For the next five years I worked on a plan to go live with Dennis. When my mom and I had real bad fights, I'd say, "Dennis, I'm coming right now. I'm making my reservations."

But during good times I'd call and say, "Dennis, I'm just going to extend my time here a little bit. I just need a little bit more time." Dennis was always understanding, but I never did make it to live with him in Seattle.

I'm 26 now. I still live in the same house as my mother and grandmother. I guess the main change is that I used to believe I could make everything work out between us. I'm not so sure about that anymore.

I'm still trying to make some major breaks from them. I've taken some steps to do so. When I first moved home, my mother did all the cooking and shopping. I was not expected to give any money. But for the last three years, I buy my own food. If I run out of something and borrow some of my mother's, I replace it.

As far as rent and expenses, no one ever talked to me about contributing, but now I pay some money toward rent.

I've made some emotional distance as well. My grandmother's sick and I spend a lot of time taking care of her. In general, though, I spend less time with my family and more time with people outside my home.

Separating from my family hasn't been easy and it's still not, but I'm not searching as much right now to figure out who I am and what I want. It took me a long time while I was in care to work through some of my own issues and believe that maybe I could change things with my family. It took me even longer to accept that maybe I can't.

In the beginning, it was painful to say that it was never going to work out. I think we all like to think that we're in control. Now I can say, "If it's not working now, it may never work." Since I've begun to accept that, I find myself happier.

After college, Tieysha attended graduate school at New York University, studying neuropsychology.

Phillip Rollano

Brotherly Love

By Jeremiyah Spears

Growing up, my brother and I were known as the twin towers. We're both very tall and we both played basketball. Lots of times we'd play together, and while I'm good, he's a bit better—well, a lot better. But whenever I missed a shot, he'd always just say, "Next time."

Other times we'd make special trips to the museum to look at the Chinese collection. My brother went to a specialized arts high school. At the museum he would sketch something so beautiful, and he'd make a copy for me.

Like all brothers, Alfred could be annoying. At night, while I was trying to do my homework, my loving brother would come in and begin to sing at the top of his lungs. He'd sing my favorite song, "One Sweet Day," by my love, Mariah Carey, or some other song, and start to tickle me when I had all this work to do.

We'd have slap fights too, and try to beat each other ferociously till we saw blood or I'd start to cry. But he'd apologize because he was a gentle person and never meant to harm me.

What I really thank my brother for the most is for being so supportive when I was having troubles. When I first began to realize I was gay, my brother always made sure I was OK—he defended me when straight guys were harassing me, and talked to me about how I was feeling, too. Basically, he helped me to get through it. One day I was home and once again I was mourning over my sexuality. I was just crying and crying. I could not stop and I felt his arms encircle me and just hold me until I couldn't cry anymore.

He always said, "No matter what you do or become you will always be my baby brutha and I'm going to love you forever." That would wipe all of my tears away and put smiles back on my face. He just held me through everything I went through: Losses, pains, anguish, and setbacks. Some nights I'd sleep in his room. We'd talk secretly about my problems. And we'd talk about his biggest problem (girls!). We talked and talked, till we drifted off to sleep.

Lots of things have been hard about being in foster care. If I had been able to be close to my brother I think my days would've been easier.

But when my mother remarried, the real problems began. My mom and brother had a lot of love for each other, but my stepdad decided that my brother and I were troublemakers. He was particularly on my brother's case. He told my mother that my brother was doing drugs and gambling, but I did not see the things he saw. I think he wanted my brother to be a saint, but my brother was just a lyrical daredevil (aka rap writer) who wanted his freedom, like all budding teenage boys do. He just wanted to hang out with friends and not run home as soon as school was over.

Still, my mom began to see it the way my stepfather saw it. She was always on our case for nothing. I couldn't believe my mom would believe her husband over her own son. I was hurt that she was putting a man before her kids.

Then one spring day it happened. My brother was tired of all the fighting and the verbal bashings, so he stayed out playing basketball till 9 p.m., which was way past his curfew. Hell got warmer when my brother walked through the door.

The memories of that night are too painful for me to describe. But eventually, my mother called the cops and had my brother arrested, and that was the last time I saw him for about a year and a half.

I didn't know where he was (turns out he was in a group home) and I cried a lot because only the good Lord knows how much I missed him. I'd lie in my bed at night and think about him and pray for his safety and strength until my tears faded away.

I missed him most when I came home to his bedroom where I sometimes slept, and he wasn't there. I missed having someone to make goofy faces with. And I missed him in my thoughts and dreams. When he first left, I used to dream about him all the time. But after not seeing him for a year, sometimes I couldn't even get a vague picture of him in my mind. The thoughts and dreams I'd had about him just vanished.

Then one day, out of the blue, my brother met me at school. I was in shock. I just stood there like I was stupid. I cut school and our graduation rehearsal to be with him. He told me everything that had happened to him, about going into care and life in his group home. He said that dealing with all the changes had been rough, and that he'd missed me too.

I was sad about all that had happened with him, but I was glad that I was with the person I loved the most. After that, though, it was a long time before I saw him again.

A couple of years after my brother went into foster care, I came to Green Chimneys, a special group home for gay kids. (I don't want to go into all the reasons why. Let's just say that as it turned out, it was really my stepfather who wasn't a saint.)

I was 15 then, and I'm 18 now. Lots of things have been hard about being in foster care, and if I had been able to be close to my brother during all this time—both when he was in care and then when both of us were in the system at the same time—I think my days would've been easier.

I'm not saying we had to live in the same group home (after all, I live in a group home for gay and transgendered teens). But I wish we'd seen each other more. Because Alfred had been like a brother, a father, and a best friend to me. But when I needed a trusted male figure to give me the answers to my problems or to help me out, he wasn't there.

I don't get to see Alfred much now. He's out of the system and he decided to move down to Mississippi, while I live here in New York City. That's a thousand miles from each other. We see each other a couple of times a year, and try to stay involved in each other's lives from a distance. But you know how that is. It's hard.

I guess I have adjusted to being without him. But I still miss him. So I wrote this in honor of my brother.

Jeremiyah was 18 when he wrote this story.
He later moved to Mississippi.

Gary Smith

Understanding Mom Helped Me Heal

By Rita Naranjo

Growing up, my mom went through a lot. She was abused both sexually and physically. She didn't have any support or encouragement and this made my mother feel like she was worthless. That feeling was hard for her to endure, and so she started using drugs. Drugs were introduced to her as a quick high that would make the pain go away. I don't think she ever could have imagined that drugs would affect her life and her future children the way they eventually did.

My mother grew up in Miami in a time when drugs weren't hard to get. In time they consumed her—mind, body, and soul, until she lost control. Because of this she had a difficult time taking care of my brothers and me.

Then my father was killed, and my mother was left devastated. She was alone, depressed, and forced to care for four young children. It was too much for her. She became even more addicted. It was her escape from the harsh realities of her life. But it led to my brothers and me being taken away from her and placed in the foster care system. I was 4 years old. Being in foster care changed my life, to say the least.

For nine years I was always in and out of the system. My mother would follow the orders of the court to get us back, but eventually she would relapse, use drugs again, and lose us. She didn't have much control over what I was doing, and I didn't care about what I was doing or about the consequences. Eventually I sort

In the beginning, each time she got clean I believed that it would last and we could be a family again.

of gave up on life. I thought, since nobody cares about me why should I care? I even ended up in juvenile hall a few times.

Each time I went into the system my main thought was how I wanted to go home and stay home. I loved my mother so much. All I could think about was being with her and my brothers. I had this deep longing inside me for so long.

In the beginning, each time she got clean I believed that it would last and we could be a family again. I was forever hopeful. Eventually I couldn't help but doubt her, because whenever I got home it wasn't long before, yep, you guessed it, right back into the system we went!

Every time this happened I became more confused, hurt and angry. I didn't understand why my mother kept making the same mistakes. So many questions entered my mind: Why was it so hard for her to stay sober and clean? Didn't my mom care? Didn't she love us and want us?

Because there wasn't anyone explaining what was going on and why, things were left open to my interpretation. I came up with my own answers and soon discovered an easy explanation. I figured that my mother must not care, love, or want us. That was the only explanation that made her behavior and addiction make sense to me.

That answer hurt me, but it also satisfied my many questions and blotted out my hopefulness. In some ways, that felt better than always hoping that everything would work out fine, and then being disappointed when it didn't. During that time, when my mom said she loved me, I couldn't say it back. I did not believe her. I had gotten to the point where I hated her. I wondered how she could say she loved me when she really didn't.

I wasn't the only one who disliked and rejected my mom because of her addiction. Everyone who dealt with my mom in any way had a strong attitude against her. I overheard some of my foster parents calling her a junkie and low life. My social worker and other people in my agency said that they didn't really care about what my mother had to say. They didn't want to hear any of her excuses, real or not. All those people just couldn't understand how she could do the things she did—get her children back only to trade them again for drugs.

The way people thought about my mom took a strong toll on me. Not only did it convince me that my mother really didn't love me, it made me feel worthless, like I was a piece of trash. My feelings and emotions were just crumpled up, stepped on and thrown away.

But little by little, as I got older, my feelings began to change. I would watch my mother in court, able to do nothing but cry. No one wanted to hear her story and she didn't know what to say, because every time she would try to explain and plead to the court, they would just close their hearts and minds.

That made me feel for my mother. It made me think that the system should be kinder to her. Though I was still angry at her, I wanted the system to give her guidance, support, and resources to help her get her life in order. I began to feel that the system helped my mom fail.

During that time, I also started thinking about my mother's

life, which had been hard, like mine. I began to realize that she still carried around pain from her childhood, which led her to use drugs to escape feeling, and which had little to do with how much she did or didn't love my brothers and me.

I also began to understand how our neighborhood contributed to her using drugs again each time she got clean. She couldn't afford to live in neighborhoods where there weren't drugs all around, so she was surrounded by temptation. My mother would always end up running into someone she knew who had drugs, and because she had an addiction, she couldn't resist.

When my mom said she loved me, I couldn't say it back. I did not believe her.

Then my brothers and I would find ourselves in a too familiar situation. Police shining their flashlights into our eyes telling us, "Wake up! You're coming with us." Then into the back of the police car, silent tears running down our faces, thoughts racing, wondering what was going to happen next.

I recognized that while my mother's addiction hurt my brothers and me, it didn't have much to do with us, and that helped make my hate toward my mother go away. But it didn't take away the hurt, and I don't think it ever will.

I still have my own pain from the past, which can come crashing back on me without warning. When it does, I hurt. I start wondering all over why my mother did the things she did. I don't think I'll ever fully understand. But even though I don't have all my questions answered, I still have gained a better understanding about my mom and her struggles, and that makes it easier for me to forgive her and move on with less pain.

Most people don't know my mother's story. They just see the things she does and judge her by that. I bet she was never given her chance to explain her side, to explain how many painful things happened in her past and how drugs were her way of giving up on a life that had never been good to her in the first place.

I'm not asking people to accept excuses from adults whose

kids are in foster care. Sometimes those things just get passed on through the generations, and it takes foster care to stop it.

The foster care system should not only keep children safe and meet their needs. They should also look out for the biological parents. After all, foster children cannot be fully helped if their parents are denied help and support. When you help the biological parents you are also helping us, their children, and ultimately helping to ensure that we will have a more positive future.

Judging biological parents won't help break the cycle of abuse, addiction, neglect, and pain. But I believe that understanding and support really can help.

Rita was 17 when she wrote this story.

Stephanie "Meadow" Kunar

Starting Over Without Them

By Hattie Rice

When I was 13, I stopped going to school. The kids called me retarded and I had no friends. All I thought about was going home to play cards and watch TV with my mom. Being at home comforting my mom was a way to get away from the torment of school and to play my role in the family—daughter and psychiatrist to my mom.

I was afraid of leaving my mother alone. I worried that one day my problems (stress and not liking people) and her problems (using drugs and hearing voices) would fall down on her and she'd die of stress.

I was 9 when my dad told me that he and my mom were schizophrenic. He was scared of people but could function. He was able to work. He said my mother had it worse. She heard voices and thought people were trying to drive her crazy and to

74

kill her. To cope with the pain, she started smoking crack.

Soon her addiction started to show. She would steal money from the family. Sometimes we'd have no food in the house and would have to go to churches or beg at the welfare office. It made me feel embarrassed. I'd think, "This is not the way a kid should live, begging for food." I felt like she didn't care about me, because if she did, why would she spend our food money on crack?

Most of the time she was high and fidgety. When I touched her, she'd jump. Other times my mother would cry because of the voices and my dad would argue with her over her drug habit.

"You going to smoke up all the money," Dad would say.

"Please, just one more smoke," Mom would say.

My brother and I used to think, "Dad, why are you letting her do this to us?"

When I stopped going to school, a typical day with my mom started with her using half of the food money on crack and then coming home and smoking it. I'd usually check on her (because I could hear her talking to the voices) and she'd tell me to tell the voices to stop hurting her. I'd say a prayer for her and we'd play her favorite card game or watch television while I held her.

Then I'd give her my usual lecture, telling her the voices are in her head and that other people

Sometimes I feel confused because I wonder, "Is it OK to feel sympathetic and angry at the same time?"

aren't doing it to her. I'd make clear that I didn't want to hurt her. I'd tell her she has a mental illness. My mom would hold me and cry when I comforted her. It was hard feeling responsible for her, and sometimes it was overwhelming because I had my own problems. I also felt it wasn't a child's place to take care of her mother.

It was especially confusing to know that my mom was not in control of the way she acted. When she took our money to buy crack, I knew it was because she felt she needed it to cope with her problems, or when I tried to touch her or get close and she'd fidget, it was because of her addiction.

I'd tell myself not to be upset, because she wasn't trying to hurt me. But as much as I tried to understand, I also felt angry and abandoned. Even now I don't think I can ever forgive my mom for spending the food money. I think to myself, "If you really loved me, why would you do that to me? You saw how I was suffering."

Over time I got depressed. When I woke in the morning, I didn't want to leave the house because I felt like the world had nothing to offer me. At home I would cry. My frustration made me start eating a lot. I used to weigh more than 185 lbs. My mother doing drugs had me feeling like life wasn't worth living. Eventually I figured I should just stay at home and avoid the world.

When I stopped going to school, I didn't think anybody would realize I was gone, but the attendance office called ACS, the child welfare agency in New York City. ACS sent a social worker to inspect our house, which was not in good shape. Every time the social worker came I stayed in my room. I think he recommended counseling for me because I would never talk to him.

The psychiatrist diagnosed me as having social phobia and I ended up being taken away from my family because they failed to make me go to school and didn't get my psychiatric prescription filled.

When I entered foster care, I was terrified. The first week, I stayed in my room and cried day and night. It was strange not to wake up and watch TV or play video games, and to have nobody to say "I love you" to. I just wanted to go back home.

Being in care felt scary because I knew my mom had nobody to console her. My parents came to visit every weekend. I felt better then because we'd go out for a walk and my mom would cry on my shoulder just like the old days.

But I soon began to feel relieved that the weight of my family's problems had been lifted off my shoulders. I realized that caring for my mom was hurting my life. I think my mom is able to get along without me. Unfortunately, that's because she smokes crack to forget about life. I feel upset about that, but it's become obvious to me that she needs more help than a child can give.

As I got settled into my placement, I realized I wasn't getting all of the attention I needed at home and it felt good to focus on myself. There was not a lot of stress in the group home and if I needed someone to talk to there was always a staff on duty. I felt good knowing I had staff that led me in the right way and girls that helped lift my spirits. That's when I started to think that foster care is where I need to be.

In the group home, I can focus on my education and try to deal with my fear of people before it gets worse. I've started interacting with the girls well (and that's never been one of my specialties) and opening up about the anger I felt toward my mom by telling a new friend what I'd been going through at home.

I felt glad that I could go see them, but I also appreciated having the option to leave when things got too intense.

During the first year of living without my parents, my depression lifted tremendously. As I talked more about my feelings and let them out, I didn't wake up crying like I did at home and I lost the weight I gained. I started to realize that the world has many wonderful things to offer me, because I started to go outside, hang out with my friends and have fun. I was even able to go back to school and keep up an 85 average.

I realized that my depression was caused by stress at home and my failure to be able to communicate with people at school and make friends. Now I know that the only worries I need to have are about me, myself, and I. It feels great to feel stronger and in control.

On my home visits, I saw that home was not where I needed to be because I saw my family still arguing over why there's no food money. Then they'd ask me for money. I'd be like, "I live in foster care and work a summer job. I ain't got no money."

I felt glad that I could go see them, but I also appreciated having the option to leave when things got too intense. I wanted to be close to my mom, to let her know I care for her and that she's not alone in this world, but I also felt like I needed to stay detached so her problems won't affect me the way they used to. Now when her problems become unbearable, it's back to my home away from home.

Not being surrounded by them has also me realize how mad I feel. I've always tried to cover up my feelings when I'm with my mom, because I figured that she has enough stress without knowing that she hurts me. But lately my feelings have been hurt so bad I can't cover them up, like when I think about how my mom and dad let us starve.

Then I blow up, screaming and yelling, "Shut the f-ck up and leave me the f-ck alone!" My mom will say, "MoMo (that's my nickname), what did I do to upset you? Why do you act like this? I love you." Instead of telling her what's wrong I'll hold her and say, "Sorry, I love you."

I only outburst once in a while but it makes me feel calm and refreshed to let my feelings out and to stand up to my mom and give her what she deserves. It's frightening, too, because sometimes I feel like I might never stop.

Since I came into foster care, I've realized how much it affects me to keep a lot of stuff held in that I need to release. Sometimes I feel confused because I wonder, "Is it OK to feel sympathetic and angry at the same time? And if I always release the sympathetic side, where is all my anger going? And if I don't want to hurt my mother, when or how will I release my rage?"

Any blind man can see that my parents want me home,

because they ask me, "When are you coming home?" and take me to my bedroom and ask me to spend a night. But whether they can actually care for me is the real question. (I think not, how about you?)

So after being in care for a year, I decided that going home would be a setback. The first person I told was my cousin. One day we were at my house and he asked me, "Do you want to come home?" Then he looked at me and added, "Who would want to come back here?" I said, "I sure as hell don't."

In July, at a meeting at my foster care agency, my social worker told my mom that I don't want to go home and my mom asked, "Is that true?" I said, "Yes." She asked, "Why, MoMo? We love you." Before she could start acting like a baby, my social worker cut her off. That day, my social worker also had my mom take a drug test. Of course she tested positive, so my social worker might try to convince her to get help.

When I left I felt good, because I felt like my mom needed to be rejected. I need to let her know I'm angry at her and that everything between us isn't peaches and cream. I feel like I'm being selfish, but I have to help myself.

I do have doubts about putting myself first, though. I wonder, "Who is my mom going to have?" And it's scary to focus on myself. Before, whenever I was confused or frustrated about my own problems, I could focus on my mom instead. Now I have nobody else's problems to get me away from my reality.

I don't think my parents really understand my decision to stay in foster care. And I think my mom is confused when I say that she's mistreated me, because she really can't seem to see what she did wrong.

For so long I never showed the way I feel about her, so I think my mom still does not understand that her drug habit affects me. Maybe the only way she'll understand is if I tell her straight up or call the police on her when she smokes or buys crack.

Right now, I think it's better for me to wonder what she knows than to know for sure, because I don't want to find out the answer. Maybe I'll have the courage to find out someday.

Hattie was 16 when she wrote this story. She graduated from high school and enrolled in college.

Jose Miguel Jimenez

Stranger to My Siblings

By Kareem Banks

I have four brothers and one sister, all younger than I am. David, who's almost 13, is the closest to me in age and hobbies. We both like sports and video games. Ellen is the only girl so I have a habit of treating her better than the others. I feel protective of my sister. James and Nicholas are both playful and full of energy. Jonathan happens to be the momma's boy because he's the youngest.

I love each and every one of them and I want to spend as much time with them as possible. I try to support them since I needed to be supported when I was their ages. Growing up in the system, I didn't get that support from my family.

I have only lived with my mother four years of my life, and the only siblings that I ever lived with were David, Ellen, and James. The group home prevented me from spending a lot of time with my siblings because I was placed very far away from them, and only got to visit on weekends or call on the phone.

When I was first placed in the group home, I felt lonely being so far away from home. Sometimes I cried from loneliness, but for the most part I was angry. When I visited my family on the weekends, it really hurt when my siblings asked when I was coming home for good, because I knew it wasn't any time soon. The more time I spent away from them, the more I felt like my sister and brothers were being stolen from me.

L ast year, when I was 17, I got discharged to my mom's house after seven years in the system. I was happy because I thought it was my chance to be a part of the family and make up for lost time. That was short-lived.

After living away from my family for so long, I didn't feel like part of it. I felt separate. My mother and I didn't know how to get along and I felt like instead of trying to establish a traditional mother and son relationship, she treated me like an outcast. Eventually she kicked me out because we argued too much.

I think that took its toll on my siblings. They were very upset.

After living away from my family for so long, I didn't feel like part of it. I felt separate.

To them, it felt like I was being stripped away from them the same way I was after a weekend visit. I felt the same way. I started to develop a natural hate for my mother and a stronger love for my siblings. Now I live with my aunt and I only see my siblings for a few hours each week. It still hurts me not to see them every day.

Just thinking about my brothers and sister is what keeps me calm. I want to protect them. I enjoy being the closest thing to a father figure that my siblings have. If I die, I'd want them to say I was the realest person they'd ever met and that I was always there for them no matter what. They make me want to do well to set a good example.

I don't just try to be an ideal big brother, but a best friend as well. I listen to them and give them advice. I walk with them in the park and help them with their homework. I teach my oldest brother how to dress fashionably, attract females, and know when to defend himself. (But I don't want him to grow up being a punk.)

Still, to be around my siblings I have to be around my mother, and we haven't found a way to make that work. Now I really wish the foster care system had placed me closer to my family when they took me away. How did they expect me to adjust to living with them, once I was almost grown?

Maybe if I'd lived closer to them all those years I was in care, I wouldn't feel like such a stranger in my mother's home. Seven years away is a long time. A lot of things changed over that time—except, in my opinion, my mother's ways. Besides being an elder brother, I don't really have a role in her home.

Kareem was 18 when he wrote this story.
He later joined the U.S. Navy.

Walter Moore

How to Make Visits Better

By Dion Jalen Buie

When my sister and I went into foster care, we were placed separately. She went to a group home and I went to a foster home. We would go to the agency to visit with my mother every Wednesday at the same time. I was really glad to see them, but I wished it was more than once a week.

At first, I didn't enjoy the visits because I didn't like the agency and there were other people around. The big tables and rolling chairs make it seem like we were in a conference room, and with other visits going on it could be very noisy.

A few months later, I was placed with an aunt in the Bronx and my sister got placed with another aunt in Harlem, in Manhattan. Our schools were only 10 blocks apart, though, so on Wednesdays, my uncle and I would go pick my little sister up from school together, and we three would go over to the ACS building and visit my mother.

I liked these visits better because my uncle was there. The four of us would talk about the situation and my mother would help us with our homework. We would sit in a cubicle that we had to ourselves, and the social worker wouldn't bother us. It was better because no one else was around.

Then they moved my sister to my grandmother's in the Bronx, near where I lived. I could go visit her at my grandmother's house and even spend the night sometimes. Four months after that, around the beginning of the school year, the court allowed me to spend weekends

Seeing my mother and my sister raises my spirits.

with my grandmother. I felt great because now I could go over there when I felt like it. My grandmother's house is very comforting because that's where I grew up.

The decision also meant I got to be around my mother more. My mom takes the bus to come see my sister and me because she now lives in Pennsylvania. She comes up two or three times a month and visits when my sister and I are both at my grandmother's house.

We get along better when we're not being watched by other people. Plus, during these visits, I don't feel like I'm in foster care. My immediate family is more positive, and everyone isn't so stressed out about this situation.

Seeing my mother and my sister raises my spirits. My sister and I talk and dance when we get together. We also go outside and we laugh and joke. When my mom visits us we talk to her about everything, and she buys us things and we just have a nice time. Sometimes it feels like I'm living with her again and we are just visiting my grandmother.

My experience shows me the way that agencies should change the way they do visits. For one thing, they should increase the amount of time you can spend with your family. If you are separated from your family, why would they only give you two hours of visitation? I would give at least four hours, because family is something special. I would also change the way the visits are planned, to make two or three visiting days a week.

Whenever it's possible, agencies should bring the children to the family's house when they have a home visit. That way, the children would always know that they have a home of their own, not just a foster home. In a family member's house you're more comfortable and you can be relaxed.

But if a visit has to be at an agency or group home, they should change the way the rooms are set up to give people privacy. You should get some alone time without anyone else looking over your shoulder. Sometimes people come in and talk with the family, and it takes time away from the visits. If I were in charge of an agency, I would block the room into sections for the visit, so you could have your own space.

And they should try to make the room feel cozier. I would have a visiting room that makes you want to be there. I'd decorate it with bright colors to brighten up minds. I'd have better furniture where you feel more at home, not rolling chairs and big tables like you're in an office meeting. I would be generous and provide a little snack because it would make the children and parents feel as if the agency really cares for people.

The experience that families have when they visit each other at an agency shouldn't feel like visiting someone in jail. The experience should feel as much as possible like being at home with your parents and brothers and sisters.

Dion wrote this story in a fall writing workshop at Represent *magazine.*

Margaret Budziar

Cut Off

By Vanessa Maldonado

One winter day, I took my mother's cocaine with me to school and told my counselor that my mother used drugs and hit me.

My counselor had wondered out loud why I showed up at school with a broken arm, stitches on my eyebrow, or my eye swollen completely shut. That made me want to tell her what was going on at my house. I figured if I told an adult, and an adult talked to my mom, she would stop taking drugs, and if she stopped taking drugs, she would stop hitting me.

By the end of the day, there were cops and social workers all over my school. They all said I had done the right thing by telling.

But the day the cops took my siblings and me away from our mother was the last day I ever spent with the people I loved most in the world—my brother, Juan, 12, and my sisters Samantha, 4, and Tiffany, 3. Because the system separated us, I have regrets and guilt about trying to make our bad situation better. Because they tore me away from everyone I ever loved, I'm sorry I opened my mouth.

The cops took us to a building for kids coming into foster care, and social workers told us that my brother would be living in another foster home. The foster mother who took my sisters and me only accepted girls. The last time I saw Juan he had his face against the cop car window, blinking back tears as my sisters and I got out to go to our new home.

A week later Juan went to live with my aunt in Buffalo. I asked my caseworker when I could see my brother again and she said, "He is not coming back, Vanessa. Face it." I was angry. How could I accept that my flesh and blood, the brother I looked up to since I was a baby, was gone? I never even had a chance to say goodbye.

My sisters and I were sent together to five different foster homes. The placements ended for various reasons: One woman got sick. Two families we loved moved back to Trinidad. One woman had to move to California because her dad got sick. (We didn't like her anyway.) Another woman pinched Tiffany, so I threw a lamp at her and that was the end of that.

Finally, my sisters and I were put with a 6' tall Puerto Rican foster mother who was loud and loved attention. Every thing was going great until she told me to call her "Mom." When I told her I was not going to, we had a big argument. She yelled, "I take in you and your sisters, and this is how you repay me—by disrespecting me!"

Instead of calling the agency, she called 911 and said I was depressed and suicidal, so I was put in Elmhurst Hospital on the psychiatric floor. I was there a little over a week. The doctors said I became depressed and antisocial because I was taken away from my mother.

When I was released, my caseworker moved me to a different foster home without my sisters. I felt like someone put my heart in a blender. I couldn't believe I was alone without them. Because of my mother's drug addiction, I had raised Tiffany and Samantha as if they were my own children, changing their diapers, feeding them every three hours, ponytailing their hair, and bathing them with Dove soap because they broke out with rashes if I used any other kind.

When we were first taken away, I thought, "At least I still have Tiffany and Samantha." I thought the good might outweigh the bad, or that I would be forgiven by God and the people in my family because I could at least make sure that Tiffany and Samantha were cared for. But now I couldn't keep them safe.

Without a father, uncles, aunts, or cousins, I was left with no connection to my past, and no real relationships. Everyone I loved had been taken away from me. Samantha and Tiffany were my main reasons to live. Now I really regretted turning in my mom.

For the next six years I was moved from foster home to foster home, from hospital to hospital. I felt empty and unloved so I would act out and push away those who cared or wanted to care. I would throw in their faces that they were not my family and never could be. (Funny, given that my own family was nothing to copy.)

I wanted to tell my brother how much I loved him and that I wished we could all be together, but I had no idea how to reach him and no one would give me his phone number. I tried to keep in contact with Tiffany and Samantha but it was hard because I moved so much. The one-hour visits ACS set up in their buildings went from once a week, to every other week, to once a month. My caseworker said the foster mother was working a lot of overtime and didn't have time to bring them to see me very often. I wondered, "How much overtime can one person do?"

During our early visits, Samantha and Tiffany hung on my every word. I would make up fairy tales about perfect families who loved each other and had super powers like reading really fast. I loved their facial expressions when something happened to the character that farted or put people to sleep. I loved how they hugged me when the story ended.

I spent the week before the visit thinking up stories they would enjoy. They weren't old enough to understand why we were put into care, so I stuck to entertaining them and making sure they had fun.

Over time I realized that my sisters were growing up and becoming interested in different things. Finally, one Wednesday when I was 14 and they were 6 and 7, I arrived at the agency building in Queens and leaned down and kissed each of them. When I called out the title of my new story they just rolled their eyes and said, "Come on, Vanessa, that's for babies."

"OK," I said, "But are y'all too old to kiss me now? Is that for babies too?"

They didn't even answer. I was so hurt.

A new reality came rushing at me. They were growing up and away from me. I was losing my position in their lives as a mother figure. What if I lost my position as their sister and best friend? What if I completely lost touch with the only people who mattered to me? Where would I fit in the world? I couldn't picture myself without Samantha and Tiffany.

Everyone I loved had been taken away from me. Now I really regretted turning in my mom.

If I lost touch with them, I would never be able to explain that they were put in care because our mother was on drugs and unable to take care of us. What if they blamed me? If they weren't in my life, everything I did to keep us together and all the sacrifices I made would be for nothing. I was also scared for them. What if they got abused and I wasn't there to help them?

Over time I became more depressed. I was diagnosed with bipolar disorder, a mental illness that causes your mood to change dramatically. I could go quickly from laughing to throwing chairs or crying. As I went in and out of mental hospitals, my visits with my sisters became less frequent. The excuses my caseworker offered for why I couldn't see them became more and more imaginative. Once she said the girls' foster mother got hit by a car. Then her mother died. I started putting things together when the caseworker used the same excuse more than once.

I figured, "Why live if I had no one left?" I felt so hopeless I tried to kill myself. For that, I was put in a mental hospital for nine months. I hated myself. I wished I had never told and had kept getting abused by my mom, just so I could hold my sisters in my arms again.

My last visit with my sisters was when they were brought to see me in the mental hospital when I was 18. Samantha was more affectionate than usual. Tiffany cried because she said Samantha was picking on her, but she wasn't.

I wonder if they knew that it was going to be the last time we would see each other. I sure didn't.

When I got out of the hospital I was placed in an apartment for teens who would be aging out of foster care soon. Immediately, I called my caseworker and asked when I could see Samantha and Tiffany.

"I don't know. I'll ask," she said. That was odd because she used to just name a time for me to show up.

A month went by and still no word. I was at a new placement and didn't want to be kicked out, so I kept my cool and kept making calls, though they seemed pointless. No one ever called me back.

In December, I received a big, thick foster care review about me, 50 pages of all the things I've been through, all of the places I went. On the last page, under the heading "status of siblings," I read, "Tiffany and Samantha have been adopted as of August 23. The adopted mother has asked that any further visitation with the biological family be canceled. No explanation was given when asked why."

The letters on the page started getting blurry. I hadn't cried in years because I never wanted to look weak, but now I sobbed. For three hours all I could do was cry, scream, and curse.

Eventually, my tears turned to action. I called everyone I could think of who might be able to help me—my ACS worker, my lawyer, and friends who could help me get through this heartbreak.

After a nap, a cold shower and a lot of support from my friends, I felt much better. I decided I was going to get my babies back. There had to be a law against this! Who gives anyone the right to prevent me from seeing my own sisters?! How could this adoptive mother have the right to split up siblings? My lawyer said, "We can go to court and fight this."

That is exactly what I did. A couple months later, I stood in front of a judge and pled my case. Six people were there, but only three were on my side. One lawyer kept bringing up the adoptive mother's right not to let "her" new kids see me.

For once, I stood up to the system that destroyed my family and found a way to put us back together again, even if it's only for three visits.

After a long debate the judge said he didn't think it was fair to split up siblings without even giving them a chance to say goodbye. He gave me three four-hour visits with Tiffany and Samantha.

Although I am not entirely satisfied, three visits is better than none, and I hope to see my sisters within the next couple months. I plan to give them all my information so they will know how to reach me after we're not allowed to see each other any more.

I don't know how I'm going to tell them on the first visit that we can only see each other two more times, or how I'll say goodbye after the last visit, but I know I have to be strong for their sake because I don't want them to be sad.

Even though I only won half the battle, I am happy that I never gave up and that something good came out of all my hard work. For once, I stood up to the system that destroyed my family and found a way to put us back together again, even if it's only for three visits.

I still need to see my brother. I've called everyone I could find in my family and found out he has joined the Marines and is stationed at Parris Island. A staff told me I can call the Red Cross to get his address. I know it is just a matter of time before I find him.

I'm still sorry I turned my mom in, but when I visit her at her apartment in Brooklyn, which I do often, I also realize she is in no shape to take care of kids. All I can do is keep working to be reunited with my brother and sisters. No one has a right to keep people who love each other apart.

Vanessa was 19 when she wrote this story.

YC Art Dept.

Paying for the Past

By Carmen Lydia Caban

On December 8, 2000, my 15-year-old son was discharged into my custody after spending a long time in a residential treatment center. I thought everything would be good. I had wanted him to come home for so long.

My children were taken from me when my son was 5, because of my drug addiction. In foster care, Luis's anger just grew and grew. He was angry at the system because he was separated from me and from his siblings. And he was angry at me because he depended on me and I let him down.

I said I would never be like my own mother, who'd neglected her children out of frustration with my father, an alcoholic. But trying to hide the scars of my past, I slipped and allowed myself to fall deep into a life of drug abuse, which in turn hurt my children.

While in care my son was fighting and threatening kids because that anger kept growing. But at 13 he began to calm down because I was finally succeeding in conquering my drug addiction. He realized that if his behavior improved, he might have a chance of coming home. He started following the rules at school and he and I attended family therapy, too. His anger was the topic we discussed most of the time.

For the first few months that my son was home, everything did seem OK. But then, suddenly, Luis became very rebellious. He felt he could stay home, not attend school, and smoke marijuana. And his anger was explosive. He would push holes in the wall and destroy property in my home. Even when he stayed to himself, I could feel that he was about to explode.

When I tried to tell Luis that he couldn't keep behaving this way, he didn't listen. Maybe he thought he had come home to the same old mother he knew before he was taken from me, the mother who got high and allowed him to do whatever he wished.

I tried to understand why my son was so angry. He would always say that he missed his sisters who I had lost parental rights for. I told him I would help him telephone them, but he would say, "You're probably just lying to me like the system did," then storm away.

Maybe he thought he had come home to the same old mother he knew before, the mother who got high and allowed him to do whatever he wished.

Probably, though he didn't say it, it was also hard for him to be home without the system to put all his anger on. He must have still just felt angry at life, and also at me, and he probably didn't know what to do with all those feelings.

As our home became crazier and crazier, with yelling and even some physical fights, I began to feel very guilty and very angry at my son for not letting me be a parent to him. I felt devastated. My main concern was that my boy was riding on a path to devastation. I wanted to tell him about the many times I put my life in danger as a teen just to get back at my own mother.

I was angry at her and I wanted her to feel pain, and the only way I knew how to do that was to make myself suffer. So I'd stepped into the streets to see all that life had to offer. I got caught up with some wild kids who could get dangerously violent in a heartbeat. I didn't want my son to suffer like I had because he couldn't deal with his anger at me. But he wasn't going to hear a lecture from me.

Eventually my son's rebellion had me so overwhelmed that I thought the system might be the only answer. I was afraid he would think I was giving up all hope in him, so I didn't ask for my son to go back into care, but I did tell the caseworker honestly about the problems we'd been having. Before long, the authorities came to pick him up because of his failure to attend school.

I replied, "My son, my rights will terminate the day I die. Until then you are stuck with me."

As he walked out the door, I held back painful tears and sorrow. I stopped Luis as the worker was taking him and said, "Luis, I love you and I'm just trying not to allow the streets to take control of my son the way it took control of Mommy."

As I watched out the window, I thought he might glance at me but he didn't. I understood. What was happening to him was his worst nightmare. It was mine, too. It felt like my past was repeating itself and I was losing one of my babies to the system once again. I just hoped that one day he would forgive me.

Then one day, after Luis had been in care a few months, the social worker called. My son had gone AWOL. I felt heart-broken. I felt like I was losing my son more and more.

A short time later, though, he showed up at my house. I kept trying to talk some sense into his young mind. Finally he said, "Mom, I respect what you are saying, but I still will not be returning to the system. I am going to take care of myself."

month and a half went by without a word from my son. Then one cold night he appeared at my friend's house. I saw my son dragging his body up the stairs. He was so exhausted he seemed intoxicated. The feelings that came over me made me stand still, numb, not knowing what to say to him. I just stared and had a flashback of my own life as a young girl in the streets.

My son said to me with a staggering voice, "Mom, I love you, I miss you. Do you love me? What did I do wrong?" He kept repeating these words over and over again. Then he said, "Can I have a hug?" I held him close to my body and embraced him as I cried silently, holding back tears.

I wanted to help my son, but I didn't want to take him back without any promises that he'd change. So I asked Luis to come upstairs and I asked my friend, "Please talk to my son, I cannot stay. I have to go."

About a week later, I received a call from the preventive worker that my son had requested a meeting. When I arrived, he said to the worker, "I want my mother to give up all her rights to being my mother." Then he turned to me and said, "So what will it be?"

I replied, "My son, my rights will terminate the day I die. Until then you are stuck with me." After that, he stormed out of the office.

A couple of months later he had a court date. I did not expect him to show up, but then I heard him whisper behind me, "Mom, is it over? What did the judge say?" I looked back at him and he looked frightened. The worker turned to me and said, "Remember, be calm. Tell him how you feel and what you would like from him. I have faith in you."

After the hearing, I asked Luis if he wanted to walk alongside me to Chinatown. He agreed. At first he only said a few words here and there, but after a while he broke down and told me what he was up to and of course it was no good. The most painful piece was when he confessed he was sleeping on the train, with no place to go and no one to turn to, just the negative associates he met along the way.

This time around, I decided, my son and I were going to make it work, even if I died trying.

He came home soon after, on March 4, 2002. For the moment, our relationship is better and so is his behavior. Every night when he comes home we talk about how his day went. He says he's working helping out a friend with cars or distributing fliers.

Living with my son is like starting all over again. Luis has had to get to know me, and I've had to get to know him.

I'm not sure I always believe him. He might be, but he also might just be playing around with his time. Still, we've made an appointment for him to start a program to get his GED and to get drug counseling, and I hope that will give him some structure in his life.

In the past, when he left his stuff around the house, I'd get mad, but now I've learned not to be bothered. When he breaks other rules, like coming home late or smoking pot, we talk about it and usually he apologizes.

After doing some soul-searching, I've also had to realize that there's a huge gap in our relationship created by those eight years that my son was in foster care. When parents and children are reunited, both sides have to face more than they bargained for.

As parents, we have to deal with our children being angry at us for failing to be someone they could always rely on. Those feelings do not go away easily. And we also have to deal with the anger we sometimes feel toward our children, even though we don't want to.

Living with my son is like starting all over again. Luis has had to get to know me, and I've had to get to know him.

---

*Carmen wrote this story in a
parent workshop at* Represent *magazine.*

Shamel Allison

A Stranger in the House

By Angel Fogah

When I was 12 years old, I went home to my mother from foster care. By age 16, it was time for me to leave again.

I never knew why I was in care as a child, and my memories of life with my mom are hazy. But I believe I moved in with my foster mother and father when I was 7 years old. My foster home was great. My foster mom and pops loved to cook. They cooked turkey wings, chicken, and my favorite, cornbread. When it got hot we'd go outside and have barbeques. I had my friends come over and play in the backyard all day. I loved it there.

After a while, I began to go see my mother on the weekends. I never felt comfortable. Some weekends were good, some were bad—it all depended on what kind of mood she was in.

If she was in a good mood she might do my hair or we might even say a few things to one another. But those times never lasted because I didn't know how to act to keep her happy. When she was in a bad mood, she'd yell or just ignore me.

I preferred my foster parents. So when my social worker told me I was going home for good, I wasn't excited. The day I left, I hugged my foster parents and tried my best not to cry while I said my last goodbye.

Life with my mother turned out to be just what I expected: She and I did not get along. My mother and my little brother had a bond going on. They went to the park, the laundromat, or the movies together. They played around or just chilled out and watched TV.

But my mother and I never had that bond. We never went shopping or cooked together or talked about how our day was. I wanted to be cool with my mom, to hang out and talk, just like she did with my little brother. But to me, she always felt like a stranger.

With all the hitting and screaming, I felt like I was an animal, trapped. This time, I wasn't going to take it.

School didn't go well, either. I had two really cool friends who were always there for me, but a lot of kids picked on me because I was small. Then one day when I was 12 years old my mother recklessly cut all my hair off. Kids started making fun of how ugly I was.

I rarely defended myself because I felt it was true—I felt small and ugly—and I didn't trust myself to fight. When I did fight I'd get so upset that I would just blank out. I was so lonely. My mother made me come straight home, but when I got home I had no one to talk to. I didn't feel comfortable talking to my mother about anything.

As time passed we had nothing but problems and more problems. My mom would scream and cuss at me about any little thing that was wrong in the house. She'd say, "You can't do anything right!" Sometimes she hit me.

My mother would also make wild accusations, like that I was

taking her socks or whatever it was that she was missing and sell-ing them to my friends. When she made these crazy accusations, I would ask myself, "Does she have some kind of problem?"

While my mother yelled, I couldn't even get two words out. I just stood there. As upset as I was, I kept quiet. I feared I might blank out on her. I would never want to hit my mother, but I feared that all the anger and the pain that I felt might one day be too much to hold in.

When I hit high school, I finally began to make some new friends and I started to like school and feel comfortable there. My friends and I would sit next to each other, or help each other out with our homework. Hanging out with my new friends made me feel free, like, "Damn, I actually have a social life." It felt so good that I could say, "Yeah, I hung out with some friends during gym and it was cool." I started to feel more confident in myself, more capable and alive.

Then one day when I got home from school my mother and I got into a really heated argument. She accused me of stealing from her. She searched me thoroughly and then hit me. With all the hitting and screaming, I felt like I was an animal, trapped. This time, I wasn't going to take it. I had reached my max. I felt like if I stayed in that house I was going to go insane.

To avoid hitting her—something I would've regretted—I just got dressed and left. I ran straight to my best friend's house, and she tended to my wounds.

I started leaving the house whenever I got upset like that. At first, I'd only stay away for a day or so. Then I would come back and my mother would make me wait outside until she felt it was time for me to come in. For hours I would sit on the stairs, waiting for her to let me in. Sometimes she wouldn't.

When she did let me in, we'd just have more arguments, so I began to leave more often. My mother wasn't providing anything a family should. She felt that I didn't deserve to sleep on a bed anymore, so she wouldn't allow me to. I could barely eat at home because she would sometimes keep the food in her bedroom or tell me, "Don't touch the food I work so hard for." I felt like life would be better anywhere besides home.

Soon my days gone began turning into weeks, and then one day I just didn't come back. I wanted to see how long it would take my mother to call the police and report me missing. I wanted to see if she really cared. She said she didn't, but I hoped that her words were hollow, that maybe she didn't mean them.

But I was in my neighborhood all the time, and not once did I see a search party. And the cops never came looking for me at school, either. I thought, "I was right—she really doesn't care." When this realization seeped into me, I felt so alone.

I wish I could find a way to have a relationship with my mom.

My life as a runaway was hard. During the day I would go to school and I would do the students' hair and charge them. For three months, this was how I made my money to eat at night. After school I would hang out with my friends, which I never got the chance to do before. It felt great to hang out and just have fun: play games at the arcade, go to the park, or just chill.

But when it got dark, I felt alone. I slept on the roof of my mother's apartment building. I dressed like a guy and was always on my guard with a blade at my side so no harm would come to me.

Out of my mother's house, I felt almost like a different person. I told my friends, "From now on, don't call me Ashley. Call me Angel." Angel was different—cooler than Ashley, and more demanding. Angel knew what to expect out of life and planned ahead. She was always in control. Angel had been growing inside me for a while, but living with my mother, I couldn't express myself freely. I liked the new me.

I soon began staying over at my friend's house during the night. It felt more like a home than my mother's home. Wrestling with her brothers, hanging out with her sisters and play fighting with their three dogs, I felt like I was a part of the family. They assured me that I was.

Then one day when I was in gym the police came and took me down to the dean's office. I was really scared. I didn't know what was going to happen to me. The police asked me how long I'd been gone, where I was staying, and other questions that I didn't really feel comfortable talking to the police about.

When they left me alone, I told my dean why I'd been gone from my house. He comforted me just by sitting there and listening to what I had to say. I was so used to not being able to tell my side of the story. It felt good to explain.

As the police filled out paperwork, I was thinking, "Man, I don't want to go back home." I was afraid that's where they might send me. My heart was beating really hard against my chest.

Finally the police handcuffed me and put me in the backseat. It was a hot day and it was hot and stuffy in the car, with no cool air coming back. The police drove me to family court, where I had to wait many hours for the judge to see me. Then I saw my mother walk in. My heart was beating so hard it hurt. I saw her look at me and just turned my head away.

Finally my case was called. I went in with my law guardian, who I had just met, and my mother, who I didn't even want to look at. Thank God that judge did not let my mom talk.

The judge decided I should spend three months in a DRC (diagnostic residential center), a temporary foster care placement where I would have to be studied to see where I belong. I was happy that I was not going to be going home. But I was still kind of worried about where I was going to be placed.

It's been a year now since I came back into the system, but things are still the same between my mom and me. I only see her in family court.

I dress nicely because I know that she will look me over from head to toe, observing everything I'm wearing. I want to show her that I can take care of myself and that I'm doing well. My mom knows how to present herself. That's one thing we have in common. So the last time I was in court I wore a pinstriped skirt with a black blouse and white pumps. I looked classy.

When I see my mom, my heart still beats fast, but not the way it did in the past. Even in court my mother tries to control me. Once my social worker wanted me to be able to go on some field trips. I needed my mom's permission, but when my worker sent the forms, she wouldn't answer. In court she said that I didn't deserve to go. (Eventually, a supervisor gave me permission.)

I told my guardian I never want to go home or have home visits. My mom hasn't fought to see me. For now, I'm trying to leave everything behind me. I don't dwell on the past. That brings back memories I don't want to remember. When I feel like memories are about to come to haunt me, I do a lot of work and exercise and think about my future and make myself forget.

But I still wonder why this happened to my mom and me. I don't understand why we never got along. We think so differently, but we do have some things in common: we both love to exercise, and we love fashion, especially shoes. But those similarities never brought us any closer.

I wish I could find a way to have a relationship with my mom. I've called her a few times since I came back into care, but she just hangs up. She holds grudges, though, so it might take a while for us to ever talk. Maybe in the future we will have a relationship, but I'm trying not to expect anything. I don't know what could bring us together. I'll just have to wait and see.

Angel was 19 when she wrote this story.

Teo Romero

Getting Back My Heart

By Daniel V.

"Why do you keep doing this to yourself?" my mother asked me with a tear rolling down her cheek. Lots of thoughts were running through my head, but I couldn't find the words to answer her question. I had just gotten arrested for shoplifting, and I was ashamed of myself.

For the past year and a half I'd been messing up my life, but I didn't realize it. Hanging out with my friends and smoking weed was like living a dream for me. I didn't have to worry about anything. Every time I got high all my stress went away.

Back then I was too stupid to realize that my friends were only there when I had money in my pocket. And I didn't notice that what I was doing was pulling my mother and me apart. I wasn't listening to her at all, and I'd rarely be home to help her.

When my mom picked me up from the precinct I felt like there was no future for me. It's hard to admit, but I was depressed. I didn't know what to expect from my mother, but she didn't give me any punishments. "This is the last chance that I'm going to give you," she said.

For the next couple of weeks I tried to stay away from negativity, but the craving for weed kept pulling me back to my friends like a magnet. And that's when my friends had this crazy idea of running away. At first I was like, "Hell no," but after a couple of blunts I didn't care.

We went to Times Square and spent a couple of days there, but after a while I was broke and tired, so I decided to go home. It was around 5:30 in the morning and I was about to get on the train when a couple of police officers stopped me and asked me for ID.

After asking me more questions they said that I had to come with them. And that's when I got really nervous. Did they have a warrant for my arrest? Did my mom report me missing? What was going on?

"I'm just going to check on you and call your parents," the cop told me. "Now sit down and be quiet." When he finally reached my mother, I felt relieved that I had someone on my side to pick me up.

It was really hard to live without my mother in my life. I could only see her twice a week, and that wasn't enough.

During their conversation I remember the cop telling my mother, "Miss, do you know that this is child neglect?" I had no idea what that meant. But then the police officer made a couple more phone calls and drove me to a strange-looking building. Some lady there started asking me tons of questions, like did my mother ever abuse me and have I ever felt suicidal.

I asked the woman what was going to happen to me next. She said that I was going to a foster home.

"Why?" I asked her with pain in my heart.

"Because," she said slowly, trying not to hurt my feelings, "Your mother doesn't want you anymore."

As soon as those words got through my brain I thought it was the end of the world. I couldn't believe it! My heart froze, and broke in a thousand little pieces.

That night I was in a group home with a whole bunch of questions, like, "What is wrong with my mother? Why would she leave me like that? Does she still love me?" I felt like I was lost on an island with no map.

A couple days later I was on my way to a foster home. I was really shy at first, and didn't want to talk to anyone about myself. Most of the time I stayed in my room, and just thought about all the wonderful times that my mother and I had spent together. I wondered how she felt saying those words to put me in care, the words that affected me so much.

When I was growing up, my mother and I were always close. My childhood in Russia was peaceful and I had lots of family around to support me. Even on bad days, being with my mom made my day turn good. I felt like she was always there whenever I needed her. And I knew that nothing would ever happen to me while I was in her arms.

But when we moved to America we were on our own, and that was hard on both of us. My mother was struggling and had to work very hard for only a few dollars. I didn't have anyone to talk to, and no big family there to love me. My mother gave me lots of love, but when she left me I was always bored and lonely.

I guess that's what pulled us away from each other. She had to work, and leave me at times, and I needed someone to be with while she was not there. I started to hang out with the wrong people and not listen to her. But I never thought it would go this far.

I wanted to apologize to my mom for causing her all this stress. I never thought of how much it hurt her. She created me and then couldn't take care of me, so that's double the pain for her. At that point I didn't know who was the failure—me, or my mother.

I felt really guilty about what I'd done and really worried about my relationship with my mother, so after a couple of days I decided to call her.

"Mom, I miss you, and I'm sorry," were the first words that came out of my mouth, and with them came tears.

"I don't know what to tell you," she said with disappointment. At that point I felt like this conversation was going to be a dead end.

"I love you, and really want to see you again," I said.

"Why did you run away?" she asked.

"I don't know," I said, trying to avoid answering.

"Well, think about it."

"I was really bored staying home all the time, and I wanted to hang out with my frie-"

Sometimes the thought of my mom leaving me again would come to my mind, and that would make me the angriest of all.

"Don't you realize that these friends of yours are leading your life to nowhere? Matter of fact, even worse than nowhere, to jail, and to growing up to be a nobody. Is that what you want to be, a nobody?" she asked me, blowing her nose.

"Of course not," I quickly answered. I promised my mom that I would be a new me, and try to succeed in life. Then I asked her the biggest question on my mind: "Why don't you want me anymore?"

After a long pause and a sigh she finally answered me. "You need a break, a break where you look at yourself and your behavior," she said. "For now I feel like I can't help you anymore. I have been trying, and my way was not working."

I begged my mom for one more chance, but she said that she'd given me plenty, and I'd messed up every one.

"Daniel, I love you with all my heart, and this is as hard for me as it is for you," she said. "But I think that this option will be best for you for now. You could have gotten locked up or even hurt. I don't want that to happen. I want you to be something in life."

I promised my mom I would try my best.

Then we talked about ways I could change my behavior. She said that the faster I improved my behavior, the faster I'd be home.

When I hung up the phone I felt much better. I knew now that my mom still cared about me. Before this phone call I thought that she wasn't ever going to speak to me again.

Even though I felt hurt by her decision, it helped me to get a hold of myself, and get back on track. I was determined to show my mother that I wasn't a failure. I felt I had the strength to improve myself, not only to get my mother back, but also to get back my positive self. I felt like it was going to be a long process, but I was ready for it.

I t was really hard to live without my mother in my life. I could only see her twice a week, and that wasn't enough. When we would see each other at my social worker's office we would talk for hours about random things, and afterwards she would take me out to eat somewhere. The first couple of times I felt strange seeing my mother, because she and I were like two different people now.

It didn't seem normal getting to know someone all over again when you'd known the person for your whole life. But I could feel that this was the best thing that I was doing for myself. Even though it was a little weird, it felt like I was getting back my heart.

Visit by visit, our relationship improved. But at times I still felt like a stranger. Sometimes we would have bad days, and with bad days came arguments. I hated arguing with the only person who loved me in America. But I couldn't control my mouth, and my anger.

I expected my mom to be less hard on me after me leaving her, but she was much stricter than before. I didn't know that learning to listen to my mother would be this hard.

Sometimes I would get angry because my mom was trying to gain control over me, and I felt that she had lost the right to control me when she put me in care. Sometimes the thought of her leaving me again would come to my mind, and that would make me the angriest of all.

I didn't want to ask my mom if she would put me in care again because I was shy, and because I really didn't want to hear her answer. Instead, I'd get angry and start arguments for no reason.

I knew that my anger was one of the things that I needed to improve if I wanted to go home. And I definitely wanted to go home. I felt that if I could live with my mother, my future would be distinguished.

So after a while I learned to overcome that fear of going back into care by telling myself that my mother would never do that to me. I also told myself that if I behaved well and listened to her, the thought wouldn't ever occur to her. I started to feel her love again, and that gave me more confidence.

The more my mother and I saw each other and talked to each other, the stronger our relationship grew. During our visits, my mother was only focused on me. I loved that feeling of knowing that someone actually cared about me. It felt good. It felt like I had someone on my side to be there for me.

In a few weeks I'll be getting discharged to my mother, and I'm not going to mess our relationship up for anything. If my mom gets a job and can't spend lots of time with me, I'll be ready for it. I've found some new friends who are more positive, and I know what could happen if I go back to the past.

I'm not the only one who has been trying to improve to make our relationship stronger. My mother is going to parenting class-es, and is trying to be the best mother that she can.

Even though we still have arguments once in a blue, we resolve them with a peaceful talk instead of screaming at each other for hours. I feel that my mother and I are a strong team now, ready for anything.

Knowing that I'm going to live with my mother again is the best feeling that I've ever experienced. The future ahead of us is a chance to build a new relationship, one that I strongly hope will last forever.

Daniel was 16 when he wrote this story. He later graduated from a military high school in Pennsylvania.

Melanie Leong

Family Life ...
After the System

Carmen Veloz is a psychologist at St. Christopher's, a foster care agency in New York City. She talked to us about how being in foster care affects parents and children.

Q: What is the effect on children of being separated from their parents?

A: Each child will react differently. Still, in general I can say that one of the most common signs is anxiety—anxiety, for one, in the form of post-traumatic stress disorder, where children will re-experience in their minds the actual separation. Some kids have recurrent nightmares, some have flashbacks of the separation.

I worked with one family where the mother had been removed by the police in handcuffs. Now one of her girls feels very threatened by the police. She says, "They're going to kill us."

I'm working with another family now. There are two boys,

8 and 10, and a girl, who's 5. In this case, after the kids were returned to their mom, they didn't want her to go to work. They were afraid she wouldn't come back. It was very hard for her to accommodate her schedule and it was hard for her to get a babysitter, too, because her kids were acting out.

Eighty percent of the kids I see also have anger-management problems. Some are depressed, which is anger turned inward. Smaller kids have a harder time because they don't have as much language development. Younger kids are much more at risk.

Q: Can children and parents work through these problems?

A: Parents ask me, "Will we ever get over this? Can I ever make it up to my child?" I tell parents that this is traumatic, but that children are very resilient. Children heal and families heal. I truly believe you can move past it.

But it also really depends on where a child is returning to. If they're returning to a household that's stronger, that's one thing. If they're returning to a home where there aren't those supports, that's another.

Reunification is a very big change, and the rules have to be renegotiated.

It's also more complicated when a child is removed at birth, because then the child doesn't form that primary attachment with the mother, and that's your strongest attachment in life. For the most part, though, if a child had secure attachment before removal, that persists.

Q: How can family therapy help parents and children build or rebuild the bridges?

A: I'm a big advocate for family therapy, because children don't operate in a vacuum. I think that, at minimum, families should have six months to a year of family therapy upon discharge. I also think families should be in therapy before the child returns, when the reunification is being planned, to prepare everyone. It's a very big change, and the rules are going to have to be renegotiated.

A lot of family therapy is just problem solving. Families come in and complain, "So and so isn't cleaning up his room." Then I'll engage the family in working together. Parents have a lot of guilt associated with the time their kids were in care, so often they don't set enough limits.

When the whole family is brought in to solve the problems, the kids feel that they have a say in the family, so they feel empowered. And parents feel that not everything has to be done by them alone, so they feel empowered.

Unfortunately, there are not enough after-care services available.

Q: What about for teen parents?

A: Teens are still developing, and suddenly they have to become adults. That's a very hard transition to make successfully. So adolescents need twice as much support.

Q: How often should parents see their children while their children are in care?

A: The only times I believe that parents shouldn't see their kids are if the abuse continues even during supervised visits, or if the parent is physically abusive in the agency. There shouldn't be a period of a few weeks where we say, "Oh well, your child was removed and we'll see what we can do."

Parents should at least have standard weekly visits to start, although my personal bias is that that is not enough. Once a parent is involved in the planning process, visitation can be increased to day visits, then overnights. But it really depends on the parent's involvement—like if the parent seeks parent support services, is in treatment, is learning parenting skills.

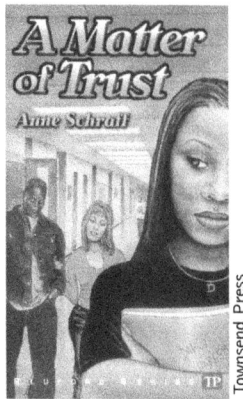

Townsend Press

A Matter of Trust

Darcy Wills clenched her hands so hard that her fingernails dug into her palms. Hakeem Randall was walking to the front of the classroom to give his English report on *Macbeth*. He was a good student, but when he got nervous, he stuttered. Darcy dreaded this moment. She knew that if he began to stutter, the class would show no mercy. Just thinking about how embarrassed he would be made her cringe.

"Oh, Tarah," Darcy whispered to her friend, "I feel so *bad* for him!"

Tarah Carson turned a stern eye on Darcy, "Girl, he gotta fight this battle himself by doin' just what he's doin', facin' it."

Darcy had been dating Hakeem for just a few weeks, but at times it seemed that she had known him forever. He was a tall, handsome boy with a lot going for him—he was a good student,

---

Here's the first chapter from *A Matter of Trust,* by Anne Schraff, a novel about teens facing difficult situations like the ones you read about in this book. *A Matter of Trust* is one of several books in the Bluford Series™ by Townsend Press.

a great singer and guitar player, and a really nice person.

"My report on *Macbeth*," Hakeem began, "is about how g-g-guilt p-pplayed an important p-p-part in the story." Darcy's worst fears were coming true. She had never heard him stutter so badly. A soft ripple of laughter began in the back row and spread around the room.

Mr. Keenan, the teacher, glared at the students. "Let's try to remember this is tenth grade English, not second grade recess!" he growled. It did not help much. Hakeem struggled on with his report, stuttering often. Stifled giggles erupted throughout the room, gurgling like an underground spring. Roylin Bailey was making a big show of covering his mouth with both hands while he rocked back and forth.

"T-t-tomorrow, and t-t-tomorrow, and t-t-tomorrow," Hakeem stammered, "creeps in this p-p-petty p-p-pace from day to day—"

"Is 't-t-tomorrow' the same thing as 'tomorrow,' Mr. Keenan?" Roylin asked cruelly. "'Cause I want to know, sir."

Tarah's boyfriend, Cooper Hodden, just shook his head while other kids laughed. Cringing, Tarah shrank down in her seat. This was as hard for Hakeem's friends to watch as it was for Hakeem to endure, Darcy thought. Then, finally, mercifully, Hakeem's report was over, and he fled to his desk like a soldier racing across a battlefield and diving into a safe ditch.

Darcy reached over and covered Hakeem's hand with hers, whispering, "It was a good report."

Hakeem pulled his hand away, anger flaring in his usually warm eyes. "I made a fool of myself," he said bitterly.

Through the rest of the class, Hakeem sat staring at his desk and fiddling so violently with his pencil that he broke it in two. Darcy knew he was reliving the humiliation of the report. He told her once that he would replay his stuttering spells over and over in his mind. His speech therapist said there was nothing really wrong with him—it was something he would eventually overcome. But not today.

When the bell rang, Darcy hurried after Hakeem. "Hakeem, it wasn't that bad, really it wasn't!" she assured him.

Hakeem slammed his fist into his open palm and shook his head. "It was stupid! I'm stupid! If I wasn't stupid, I could talk right!"

"Hey man," Cooper said, standing in front of the snack machines, "don't sweat it. We all feel stupid sometimes. Once, I gave an oral presentation, and people were laughing but I didn't know why. Then the teacher whispered to me that my fly was unzipped."

"Yeah, and he was wearin' bright red boxer shorts that day," Tarah chimed in, smirking.

Hakeem jammed change into the soda-machine slot. He yanked out the can and walked away without saying anything. When Darcy tried to follow him, Tarah grabbed her wrist. "Girl," Tarah scolded, "give it a rest. We all got our lumps and bumps, and nobody gets outta this world without bein' banged up. It's not the end of the world that Hakeem messed up on a report. Let him work it out his own self."

Darcy reluctantly let Hakeem walk down the corridor alone. She felt so bad for him. Right now he was hating himself, and she understood that. Darcy had hated herself all through middle school and her first year at Bluford High because boys just seemed to ignore her. Every other girl in her class seemed prettier, more popular, and Darcy's shyness hurt something like Hakeem's stutter must have.

Darcy walked slowly towards the library to work on a science report. Her father had offered to take her to the Palomar Observatory for the report. The observatory would have made a great topic, but Darcy turned him down. Her father had been away from the family for five years, and now he was trying to rebuild his relationship with them. But Darcy felt awkward and strange with him.

Now she felt estranged from Hakeem too. He was hurting so much, and he would not let her try to help.

As Darcy reached the library, she noticed a flyer posted on the door:

Talent show auditions.
February 20, Noon.
Singers, musicians, dancers, artists.

The depressing thoughts of a moment ago were suddenly forgotten. Darcy's heart raced with excitement over what this could mean for Hakeem.

Everyone knew he was a great guitar player and a wonderful singer. When he sang, he never stuttered. Darcy could not wait till school was over so she could track him down. This show was just what he needed to boost his spirits.

After school, Darcy found Hakeem sitting under the pepper tree behind the Bluford parking lot. His guitar was resting on his lap. She sat beside him on the grass and said, "Did you hear about the auditions for the talent show? You'd be just great for that, Hakeem. You'd blow 'em away!"

"Yeah, watch the stuttering idiot perform. Maybe I could do a ventriloquist act so the kids'll think the dummy is the one who stutters!" Hakeem said bitterly.

"But you don't stutter when you sing," Darcy pointed out.

"I guess," he said, rolling a red berry between his fingers and watching the papery skin pop off, leaving a little brown seed. "Why don't *you* audition, Darcy? You have a nice singing voice. And you don't stutter."

"Oh, I'm no singer," Darcy blushed. " Sure you are," Hakeem insisted. "I've heard you. And you told me you used to sing in a church choir."

"But that's because Mom made me."

"Well, you should really enter this contest. It might give you that spark to start singing again."

"I will if you will," Darcy said impulsively, though the very thought of performing before the student body made her shudder.

Hakeem finally smiled. "Okay. Deal. Maybe we'll both make such fools of ourselves we'll have to run away to a desert island and hide."

Darcy glanced at her watch. A neighbor, Ms. Harris, was sitting with Darcy's grandmother, but Darcy still had to be home soon. "Gotta go now," she said. "Grandma will be needing me."

"How is she?" Hakeem asked.

Darcy shrugged. Grandma hadn't been well since her stroke a year and a half ago. "She's about the same. Some days, she's, you know, almost like normal for a few hours, and then she's back to thinking she's a little girl in her mom's house. I think she always knows me. I mean, she calls me 'Angelcake,' and she's always got a smile for me."

"Your parents getting any closer?" Hakeem asked.

"Dad goes down to the hospital where Mom works, and sometimes they talk in the cafeteria. I don't know if Mom would ever let him come back or even if he wants to. He's just trying to make up for what happened, you know, for running out on us."

"You want your parents together again, Darcy?"

"I don't know. Dad gets along good with Jamee. Even when we were little, she was always closer to him than I was. Maybe it's because she's two years younger than me, and Dad was always ready to baby her. I think right now she's ready to forgive him, but I can't say I am ready to do that. Maybe I should, but it's hard," Darcy admitted.

Hakeem gave Darcy a quick hug. "Like Tarah is always saying, 'We gotta make the best of what we got 'cause there ain't nothin' else to do!'"

They both laughed, and Hakeem picked up his guitar. He strummed a melody and began to sing in his rich, deep voice:

Will you hear me if I cry,
Above the thunder of anger,
Over blasts of fear and hate,
When help comes not at all,
Or when it comes too late?
When streets explode with fire,
And hearts grow dead with grief,
When all the sounds are sad,
And there's no more relief?
Will you hear me if I cry?
Will you come before I die?

"Did you just write that?" Darcy asked.

"A couple of weeks ago. I was visiting my cousins, and we were talking about Russell Walker, that guy who went down in a drive-by shooting last year. I sort of wrote it for him."

"Yeah, I heard about him," Darcy said. "He was an honor student and an athlete, wasn't he?"

Hakeem nodded somberly.

"That was a crying shame," she added. "I hope they catch the guys who did it and put them behind bars for good."

Darcy was heading home when she ran into Brisana Meeks. Until just a few weeks ago, they had been best friends. When Darcy started hanging out with Tarah, Cooper and their friends, Brisana cut off the friendship. Since then, Darcy had made small efforts to repair their relationship. "Hey, Brisana," Darcy said, "how's it going?"

"Terrific," Brisana said with a sharp edge to her voice. Brisana had once told Darcy that she and Darcy were the bright, sophisticated kids at Bluford High. They were the "tens." It was their duty to avoid the low-class, stupid kids like Tarah and Cooper, who were zeroes.

"Want to go to the mall on Saturday, Brisana?" Darcy asked.

"With *you?*" Brisana scoffed, placing her hands on her hips. "No thanks," she added, leaving Darcy speechless.

As Darcy walked on, Roylin Bailey pulled up alongside her in a teal-blue Honda. "Hey Darcy, want a lift?" he shouted.

"No, thanks," Darcy said.

"Come on, Darcy," Roylin persisted. "Why are you wastin' your time with that stuttering fool? Sistah, I'm here to tell you, he ain't the one."

"Roylin, leave me alone. I don't remember asking for your opinion on my social life," Darcy snapped.

"Relax, girl. I'm just tryin' to help you out. You know, pass on the male perspective. And from where I'm sittin' you could do a lot better than Ha-ke-keke-keem," he said, snickering.

Out of the corner of her eye, Darcy saw Cooper Hodden's beat-up truck roll up behind the Honda. Tarah, sitting beside Cooper, yelled, "Cooper, baby, you know your brakes ain't so good. Don't go smashin' that Honda now!"

"I can't stop!" Cooper howled, hitting the horn and blasting Roylin's Honda out of his path. Both Cooper and Tarah doubled over laughing as Roylin sped away.

"You guys are outta your minds!" Darcy said, also laughing. "Thanks, I owe you." Leaning in the truck window, she confided, "Hey, guess what. I told Hakeem I'd sign up for the talent show that's coming up, just to make him try out. Problem is, I'm terrified of getting up in front of all those people. And then there's the issue of my voice."

"What's wrong with your voice?" Cooper asked. "You talkin' okay right now."

"No, my *singing* voice. It doesn't exactly make people jump to their feet with applause. Fall to their knees begging me to stop, maybe, but not jump to their feet," Darcy said.

"Girl, don't even worry about it," Tarah advised. "Just play the music real loud, smile real pretty, and nobody'll notice how you sing."

"Thanks, I'll keep that in mind," Darcy replied sarcastically.

Darcy climbed into the cramped front seat of the pickup truck for a ride home just as Hakeem sped by on a shiny silver motorbike. Hakeem did not seem to notice Darcy, but she saw him—with Brisana Meeks sitting behind him with her arms around his waist.

"That's weird," Darcy said. "I haven't even seen his new bike, and there she is riding on it."

"He prob'ly just givin' her a lift," Tarah said.

"Don't know about that," Cooper chimed in. "That girl's *fine*."

Tarah nudged Cooper in the ribs with her elbow, and he howled. But the damage was done. It was done the minute Darcy saw Brisana riding on Hakeem's motorbike.

"Brisana always used to make fun of Hakeem because he stuttered," Darcy said.

"Stuck-up girl like her, she prob'ly just going after him to mess with your head," Tarah replied.

Or maybe, Darcy thought, *I like Hakeem a lot more than he likes me.* A cold chill pressed down on Darcy's chest like a heavy blanket of ice.

Teens:
How to Get More Out of This Book

Self-help: The teens who wrote the stories in this book did so because they hope that telling their stories will help readers who are facing similar challenges. They want you to know that you are not alone, and that taking specific steps can help you manage or overcome very difficult situations. They've done their best to be clear about the actions that worked for them so you can see if they'll work for you.

Writing: You can also use the book to improve your writing skills. Each teen in this book wrote 5-10 drafts of his or her story before it was published. If you read the stories closely you'll see that the teens work to include a beginning, a middle, and an end, and good scenes, description, dialogue, and anecdotes (little stories). To improve your writing, take a look at how these writers construct their stories. Try some of their techniques in your own writing.

Reading: Finally, you'll notice that we include the first chapter from a Bluford Series novel in this book, alongside the true stories by teens. We hope you'll like it enough to continue reading. The more you read, the more you'll strengthen your reading skills. Teens at Youth Communication like the Bluford novels because they explore themes similar to those in their own stories. Your school may already have the Bluford books. If not, you can order them online for only $1.

Resources on the Web

We will occasionally post Think About It questions on our website, www.youthcomm.org, to accompany stories in this and other Youth Communication books. We try out the questions with teens and post the ones they like best. Many teens report that writing answers to those questions in a journal is very helpful.

How to Use This Book in Staff Training

Staff say that reading these stories gives them greater insight into what teens are thinking and feeling, and new strategies for working with them. You can help the staff you work with by using these stories as case studies.

Select one story to read in the group, and ask staff to identify and discuss the main issue facing the teen. There may be disagreement about this, based on the background and experience of staff. That is fine. One point of the exercise is that teens have complex lives and needs. Adults can probably be more effective if they don't focus too narrowly and can see several dimensions of their clients.

Ask staff: What issues or feelings does the story provoke in them? What kind of help do they think the teen wants? What interventions are likely to be most promising? Least effective? Why? How would you build trust with the teen writer? How have other adults failed the teen, and how might that affect his or her willingness to accept help? What other resources would be helpful to this teen, such as peer support, a mentor, counseling, family therapy, etc.?

Resources on the Web

From time to time we will post Think About It questions on our website, www.youthcomm.org, to accompany stories in this and other Youth Communication books. We try out the questions with teens and post the ones that they find most effective. We'll also post lessons for some of the stories. Adults can use the questions and lessons in workshops.

Discussion Guide

Teachers and Staff:
How to Use This Book in Groups

When working with teens individually or in groups, you can use these stories to help young people face difficult issues in a way that feels safe to them. That's because talking about the issues in the stories usually feels safer to teens than talking about those same issues in their own lives. Addressing issues through the stories allows for some personal distance; they hit close to home, but not too close. Talking about them opens up a safe place for reflection. As teens gain confidence talking about the issues in the stories, they usually become more comfortable talking about those issues in their own lives.

Below are general questions to guide your discussion. In most cases you can read a story and conduct a discussion in one 45-minute session. Teens are usually happy to read the stories aloud, with each teen reading a paragraph or two. (Allow teens to pass if they don't want to read.) It takes 10-15 minutes to read a story straight through. However, it is often more effective to let workshop participants make comments and discuss the story as you go along. The workshop leader may even want to annotate her copy of the story beforehand with key questions.

If teens read the story ahead of time or silently, it's good to break the ice with a few questions that get everyone on the same page: Who is the main character? How old is she? What happened to her? How did she respond? Another good starting question is: "What stood out for you in the story?" Go around the room and let each person briefly mention one thing.

Then move on to open-ended questions, which encourage participants to think more deeply about what the writers were feeling, the choices they faced, and the actions they took. There are no right or wrong answers to the open-ended questions.

Open-ended questions encourage participants to think about how the themes, emotions, and choices in the stories relate to their own lives. Here are some examples of open-ended questions that we have found to be effective. You can use variations of these questions with almost any story in this book.

—What main problem or challenge did the writer face?

—What choices did the teen have in trying to deal with the problem?

—Which way of dealing with the problem was most effective for the teen? Why?

—What strengths, skills, or resources did the teen use to address the challenge?

—If you were in the writer's shoes, what would you have done?

—What could adults have done better to help this young person?

—What have you learned by reading this story that you didn't know before?

—What, if anything, will you do differently after reading this story?

—What surprised you in this story?

—Do you have a different view of this issue, or see a different way of dealing with it, after reading this story? Why or why not?

Credits

The stories in this book originally appeared in the following Youth Communication publications:

"Cut Off," by Vanessa Maldonado, *Represent*, May/June 2006; "A Mother to Me," by Roger Griffin, *Represent*, May/June 2006; "Finding Our Way Home," by Janelle Allen, *Represent*, March/April 2008; "'It Won't Happen Again,'" by Youshell Williams, *Rise*, November 2007; "A Safe Place to Connect," *Rise*, Summer 2006; "Letting the World Back In," by Anonymous, *Represent*, March/April 2008; "Torn Apart," by Anonymous, *Represent*, January/February 2009; "Loving Letters," by Erica H., *Represent*; September/October 2006; "Too Far From Mom," by Chris Brooks, *Represent*, September/October 2001; "Going Home Again," by Tieysha, *Represent*, January/February 2001; "Brotherly Love," by Jeremiyah Spears, *Represent*, July/August 2000; "Understanding Mom Helped Me Heal," by Rita Naranjo, *Represent*, November/December 2001; "Starting Over Without Them," by Hattie Rice, *Represent*, March/April 2004; "Stranger to My Siblings," by Kareem Banks, *Represent*, September/October 2003; "How to Make Visits Better," by Dion Jalen Buie, *Represent*, January/February 2009; "Starting Over," by Christiaan Perez, *Represent*, January/February 2005; "Paying for the Past," by Carmen Lydia Caban, *Represent*, July/August 2002; "A Stranger in the House," by Angel Fogah, *Represent*, March/April 2008; "Getting Back My Heart," by Daniel V., *Represent*, May/June 2008; "Family Life . . . After the System," *Represent*, January/February 2000.

About
Youth Communication

Youth Communication, founded in 1980, is a nonprofit youth development program located in New York City whose mission is to teach writing, journalism, and leadership skills. The teenagers we train become writers for our websites and books and for two print magazines: *New Youth Connections*, a general-interest youth magazine, and *Represent*, a magazine by and for young people in foster care.

Each year, up to 100 young people participate in Youth Communication's school-year and summer journalism workshops, where they work under the direction of full-time professional editors. Most are African-American, Latino, or Asian, and many are recent immigrants. The opportunity to reach their peers with accurate portrayals of their lives and important self-help information motivates the young writers to create powerful stories.

Our goal is to run a strong youth development program in which teens produce high quality stories that inform and inspire their peers. Doing so requires us to be sensitive to the complicated lives and emotions of the teen participants while also providing an intellectually rigorous experience. We achieve that goal in the writing/teaching/editing relationship, which is the core of our program.

Our teaching and editorial process begins with discussions

between adult editors and the teen staff. In those meetings, the teens and the editors work together to identify the most important issues in the teens' lives and to figure out how those issues can be turned into stories that will resonate with teen readers.

Once story topics are chosen, students begin the process of crafting their stories. For a personal story, that means revisiting events in one's past to understand their significance for the future. For a commentary, it means developing a logical and persuasive point of view. For a reported story, it means gathering information through research and interviews. Students look inward and outward as they try to make sense of their experiences and the world around them and find the points of intersection between personal and social concerns. That process can take a few weeks or a few months. Stories frequently go through 10 or more drafts as students work under the guidance of their editors, the way any professional writer does.

Many of the students who walk through our doors have uneven skills, as a result of poor education, living under extremely stressful conditions, or coming from homes where English is a second language. Yet, to complete their stories, students must successfully perform a wide range of activities, including writing and rewriting, reading, discussion, reflection, research, interviewing, and typing. They must work as members of a team and they must accept individual responsibility. They learn to provide constructive criticism, and to accept it. They engage in explorations of truthfulness, fairness, and accuracy. They meet deadlines. They must develop the audacity to believe that they have something important to say and the humility to recognize that saying it well is not a process of instant gratification. Rather, it usually requires a long, hard struggle through many discussions and much rewriting.

It would be impossible to teach these skills and dispositions as separate, disconnected topics, like grammar, ethics, or assertiveness. However, we find that students make rapid progress when they are learning skills in the context of an inquiry that is personally significant to them and that will benefit their peers.

When teens publish their stories—in *New Youth Connections* and *Represent*, on the Web, and in other publications—they reach tens of thousands of teen and adult readers. Teachers, counselors, social workers, and other adults circulate the stories to young people in their classes and out-of-school youth programs. Adults tell us that teens in their programs—including many who are ordinarily resistant to reading—clamor for the stories. Teen readers report that the stories give them information they can't get anywhere else, and inspire them to reflect on their lives and open lines of communication with adults.

Writers usually participate in our program for one semester, though some stay much longer. Years later, many of them report that working here was a turning point in their lives—that it helped them acquire the confidence and skills that they needed for success in college and careers. Scores of our graduates have overcome tremendous obstacles to become journalists, writers, and novelists. They include National Book Award finalist and MacArthur Fellowship winner Edwidge Danticat, novelist Ernesto Quiñonez, writer Veronica Chambers, and *New York Times* reporter Rachel Swarns. Hundreds more are working in law, business, and other careers. Many are teachers, principals, and youth workers, and several have started nonprofit youth programs themselves and work as mentors—helping another generation of young people develop their skills and find their voices.

Youth Communication is a nonprofit educational corporation. Contributions are gratefully accepted and are tax deductible to the fullest extent of the law.

To make a contribution, or for information about our publications and programs, including our catalog of over 100 books and curricula for hard-to-reach teens, see www.youthcomm.org.

About the Editors

Laura Longhine is the editorial director at Youth Communication, where she oversees editorial work on the organization's books, websites, and magazines. She edited *Represent*, Youth Communication's magazine by and for teens in foster care, for three years.

Prior to joining Youth Communication, Longhine was as a staff writer at the *Free Times*, an alt-weekly in South Carolina, and a freelance reporter for various publications. Her stories have been published in *The New York Times*, *Legal Affairs*, newyorkmetro.com, and *Child Welfare Watch*. She has a bachelor's in English from Tufts University and a master's in journalism from Columbia University.

Longhine is the editor of several other Youth Communication books, including *Watching My Parents Disappear: Teens Write About Living with Drug Addiction* and *Analyze This! A Teen Guide to Therapy and Getting Help*.

Keith Hefner co-founded Youth Communication in 1980 and has directed it ever since. He is the recipient of the Luther P. Jackson Education Award from the New York Association of Black Journalists and a MacArthur Fellowship. He was also a Revson Fellow at Columbia University.

More Helpful Books
From Youth Communication

Do You Have What It Takes? A Comprehensive Guide to Success After Foster Care. In this survival manual, current and former foster teens show how they prepared not only for the practical challenges they've faced on the road to independence, but also the emotional ones. Worksheets and exercises help foster teens plan for their future. Activity pages at the end of each chapter help social workers, independent living instructors, and other leaders use the stories with individuals or in groups. (Youth Communication)

The Struggle to Be Strong: True Stories by Teens About Overcoming Tough Times. Foreword by Veronica Chambers. Help young people identify and build on their own strengths with 30 personal stories about resiliency. (Free Spirit)

Depression, Anger, Sadness: Teens Write About Facing Difficult Emotions. Give teens the confidence they need to seek help when they need it. These teens write candidly about difficult emotional problems—such as depression, cutting, and domestic violence—and how they have tried to help themselves. (Youth Communication)

What Staff Need to Know: Teens Write About What Works. How can foster parents, group home staff, caseworkers, social workers, and teachers best help teens? These stories show how communication can be improved on both sides, and provide insight into what kinds of approaches and styles work best. (Youth Communication)

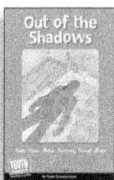

Out of the Shadows: Teens Write About Surviving Sexual Abuse. Help teens feel less alone and more hopeful about overcoming the trauma of sexual abuse. This collection includes first-person accounts by male and female survivors grappling with fear, shame, and guilt. (Youth Communication)

Just the Two of Us: Teens Write About Building Good Relationships. Show teens how to make and maintain healthy relationships (and avoid bad ones). Many teens in care have had poor role models and are emotionally vulnerable. These stories demonstrate good and bad choices teens make in friendship and romance. (Youth Communication)

The Fury Inside: Teens Write About Anger. Help teens manage their anger. These writers show how they got better control of their emotions and sought the support of others. (Youth Communication)

Always on the Move: Teens Write About Changing Homes and Staff. Help teens feel less alone with these stories about how their peers have coped with the painful experience of frequent placement changes, and turnover among staff and social workers. (Youth Communication)

Two Moms in My Heart: Teens Write About the Adoption Option. Teens will appreciate these stories by peers who describe how complicated the adoption experience can be—even when it should give them a more stable home than foster care. (Youth Communication)

My Secret Addiction: Teens Write About Cutting. These true accounts of cutting, or self-mutilation, offer a window into the personal and family situations that lead to this secret habit, and show how teens can get the help they need. (Youth Communication)

Growing Up Together: Teens Write About Being Parents. Give teens a realistic view of the conflicts and burdens of parenthood with these stories from real teen parents. The stories also reveal how teens grew as individuals by struggling to become responsible parents. (Youth Communication)

To order these and other books, go to:
www.youthcomm.org
or call 212-279-0708 x115

CPSIA information can be obtained
at www.ICGtesting.com
Printed in the USA
BVHW06s0440181018
530452BV00010B/727/P